Tumbling and Balancing for All

Second Edition

George Szypula

Michigan State University

WM. C. BROWN COMPANY PUBLISHERS
Dubuque, Iowa

Copyright © 1957 by
George Szypula

Copyright © 1968 by
Wm. C. Brown Company Publishers

Library of Congress Catalog Card Number: 68—19713

ISBN 0—697—07310—6

Tenth Printing, 1970

Printed in the United States of America

Dedication

This book is dedicated to my parents, to the late
Professor William J. Herrmann, Sr. who was my
instructor, to my wife, June, and our children,
Cheryl, George, Carl, and Susie.

The Author at a Tender Age

Championships Won

SENIOR MIDDLE ATLANTIC A.A.U. TUMBLING—1935, 1936, 1937, 1938, 1939, 1940, 1941, 1942, 1943, 1946.

EASTERN INTERCOLLEGIATE ALL AROUND GYMNASTIC—1942, 1943.

NATIONAL COLLEGIATE TUMBLING—1943.

NATIONAL A.A.U. TUMBLING—1940, 1941, 1942, 1943.

PRESIDENT OF NATIONAL ASSOCIATION OF GYMNASTICS COACHES—1957.

N.C.A.A. TEAM CHAMPIONS—1958.

GYMNASTICS COACH OF THE YEAR—1966.

ASSOCIATE PROFESSOR PHYSICAL EDUCATION—GYMNASTICS COACH SINCE 1947 AT MICHIGAN STATE UNIVERSITY.

COACHED 38 BIG TEN AND 16 NATIONAL INDIVIDUAL CHAMPIONS.

Foreword to the Second Edition

TUMBLING AND BALANCING FOR ALL is an American gymnastic classic. It is one of the most frequently mentioned references on the subject George Szypula knows so well. As a National Champion and an excellent teacher—an admirable combination even if you don't write a book—George has willingly shared his wealth of knowledge with the gymnastic community.

Applications of the text are valuable for men and women. George was one of few men who was honored by participation in both the First and Second National Institutes on Girls' Sports sponsored by the Olympic Development Committee and the Division of Girls' and Women's Sports of the American Association for Health, Physical Education and Recreation.

He has also been a driving force in planning for and directing the National Summer Gymnastic Clinic at his home base of Michigan State University, where he is the varsity gymnastic coach.

Most of us who know George would additionally say that the only better source than his book is the man himself. If George is on the program some time, go listen to him. His personal magnetism, Philadelphia humor and ability to handle with equal finesse the little preschooler and the intercollegiate gymnastic champion are remembered by his audiences and friends.

I sincerely hope that this new edition of TUMBLING AND BALANCING FOR ALL, which contains additional material in floor exercise, triple balancing and pyramid building, is well used and applied by all of us who would emulate a real pro...George Szypula.

A. Bruce Frederick
Education Editor
THE MODERN GYMNAST

Foreword to the First Edition

There is a vast and as yet unfulfilled need for a book in gymnastics which has the basics of all apparatus defined and explained. Work is now being done on this nomenclature and terminology by a committee with Frank Cumiskey as chairman appointed by the National Gymnastics Clinic at Sarasota, Florida. George Szypula is making a major contribution in the field of tumbling, balancing, and related activities. With his wonderful record of four times N.A.A.U. Tumbling champion plus his outstanding record as gymnastics coach of Michigan State University, he is sure to have a maze of valuable information.

His techniques of stunt explanation and analysis should do much for the beginner as well as the advanced in making learning easier and more correct. The progressions in these fields are of most importance and should insure correct performance and practice which will help the safety aspect of these activities. Mr. Szypula's patterns for performance are readable and exact in the nature of the progressions he has listed. His picture tables will be valuable for the coach, teacher, and pupil and performer.

I heartily recommend this book as a valuable aid in our never ending search for better, more efficient ways of teaching and training in our gymnastics progressions. With the increased interest in gymnastics we need a book of this type and the reader will find many valuable aids for improving the existing faults in his performance.

Charlie Pond

Charlie Pond
Gymnastics Coach
University of Illinois

Acknowledgments

Many people helped with the writing of his book, and I should like to acknowledge their efforts.

I am grateful to:

Jerry Gildemeister, one of my former students, and Dave Laura, a student at Michigan State, for their photographic work.

Joe Schabacker, my former teammate, and his partner, Al Motter, who supplied me with most of the advanced handbalancing stunts. These excellent pictures added greatly to the balancing section.

Charlie Pond, who granted me permission to use pictures of his former national tumbling champions, Bob Sullivan and Dick Browning.

James "Corky" Sebbo for the trouble he went to in supplying me with pictures of some of his tumbling routines.

Bud Bronson, who, along with Jerry, appeared in many of the pictures.

Bonnie Lackey, a student at Michigan State, for her art work.

Department of Sports Information at Michigan State University for use of their cheerleading photos.

Vic Krumdick for his fine handbalancing shots of himself and his young performers.

And also all the others who appear in the book:

Sue Adams	Jan Govan	Dorothy Schabacker
Cherry Almy	Ben Gunning	Loa Sheridan
Ron Aure	Chris Harner	Dennis Smith
Jake Baumgartner	Merry Jo Hill	Carl Szypula
Dick Becker	George Hopely	Cheryl Szypula
Iraj Behbehani	Mark Kruger	George Szypula
Jim Breza	Tom Kuhlman	June Szypula
Roland Brown	Don Leas	Susie Szypula
William Coco	Gloria Levins	Jim Tait
Jim Curzi	Raeanne Miller	Dave Thor
Mike Devaney	Dave Mohre	Toby Towson
Craig Fedore	Dick O'Brien	Don Vest
Michelle Fry	Jim Parker	John Walker
Goodrich and Nelson	Carl Rintz	Harry Wilkinson

Introduction

WHY TUMBLING?

Because of various misconceptions about tumbling, many schools, private clubs and other organizations fail to include it in their physical education programs. One common complaint is that equipment costs too much; however, the cost of four tumbling mats, twenty feet long and five feet wide, sufficient for the ordinary program, is just slightly more than the cost of most equipment needed for other sports. When properly cared for, good mats will last a long time; under normal use, they should last about ten years. Consider also that mats can be used for wrestling—another valuable physical education activity. If the cost of mats still seems prohibitive, remember that in a well-rounded physical education program almost everyone, including girls, will participate in tumbling to some extent. This can be said for few varsity sports.

A second argument claims that tumbling is too dangerous. Actually, it is dangerous only if the equipment, instruction and supervision are inadequate. But practically every sport is dangerous under such conditions. A program adapted to the ability level of the participants should not be hazardous. The novice, challenged by elementary stunts, should find his experience a safe one.

Finally, there is the argument that many physical education instructors are not competent enough to teach tumbling. This point appears to be the most valid of the three, yet even this can be remedied rather easily. Colleges could require their physical education majors to take more course work in tumbling. Most colleges require a two- or three-hour course, which probably should be increased. Even this amount of course work could provide sufficient training to handle the ordinary tumbling satisfactorily, particularly if the teacher is willing to spend a little time reviewing the subject. The course work should be supplemented by a comprehensive, well-illustrated reference book; this book has been written for his purpose. It is also designed for students who, without the services of a teacher, must teach one another. Clubs, recreation centers and other organizations could easily overcome any incompetency by enlisting the aid of capable local individuals as consultants and assistants to the regular instructors responsible for the total program.

There are numerous reasons which justify the inclusion of tumbling in a physical education program. Like any good sport, it provides healthful exercise and develops cooperation and good sportsmanship. Since many stunts are performed individually, it also develops a student's self-reliance. It is also the backbone of all gymnastics; most movements learned in tumbling can be incorporated into performances on the apparatus. Moreover, by training the student to perform intricate body movements skillfully, tumbling develops the body control and coordination basic to many sports. As in other sports, the tumbler has the opportunity to perform in demonstrations and shows as an amateur, as a competitor on an intramural or on an extramural level (regardless of his size) or as a professional entertainer.

Table of Contents

Figures

Tumbling and Balancing for All

Chapter 1

Responsibilities of Instructors and Students

INSTRUCTOR'S RESPONSIBILITIES

<u>Assistance</u>

This word refers to the help that one or two persons provide for one or two tumblers and balancers during the performance of stunts with or without mechanical devices. It will be used synonymously with the word <u>spotting</u>.

The instructor's most important job is to assist students while they perform stunts. Until he gains proficiency, he should practice assistance techniques as diligently as his students practice tumbling and balancing. Through spotting he can protect and instill confidence in them during their early attempts. By teaching spotting techniques to his students he can get them to spot one another with or without his help.

(1) Hand Spotting

Later the various types of hand spotting will be presented fully under the stunts for which they are employed.

(2) Hand-Belt Spotting

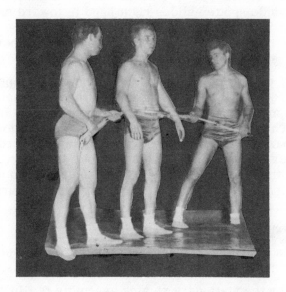

Performer stands in center of mat with either a flat safety belt or a Pond* twisting belt around his waist. It is shown in Figure 1 on the following page. On either side of the

---

* The Pond twisting belt was developed by Charlie Pond.

1

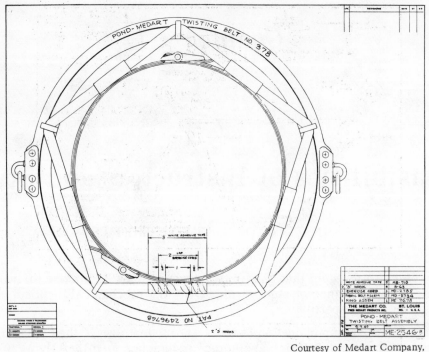

Courtesy of Medart Company,
St. Louis, Missouri.

Figure 1

belt is a five-foot rope attached by means of a swivel. This attachment allows the tumbler to turn over forward or backward without a hitch.

Spotter at left side of performer grasps rope with left hand about two feet from swivel and right about twelve inches closer than left to swivel. Spotter at right side does the opposite.

Tumbler runs down mat with spotters a little ahead of him. As he reaches an upside-down position, left-side spotter slides right hand in toward tumbler's waist and steps in with his right foot. Spotter on other side does the opposite. This puts them in position to support performer if he cannot complete somersault properly. After tumbler completes somersault, spotters ease him to mat.

In the twisting belt, performer can do the Roundoff-19 unimpeded and twist as many rotations as possible around the longitudinal axis on the somersault. In a flat belt he has to turn it to the right so the left-side spotter's rope is in front of him and the right-side spotter's rope is behind him. As he turns left for the roundoff, his ropes will return to the starting position, and he will be ready to tumble backward down the mat. In forward tumbling, performer can run down the mat without difficulty. For twisting in the Forward Somersault-44 use the Pond twisting belt. It consists of two metal rings, one inside the other separated by ball bearings, permitting inner ring to turn freely and allowing performer to twist unimpeded.

(3) Overhead Suspension-Belt Spotting

There are two types of overhead suspension for the safety belt, the stationary and the traveling rigging system.

The erection plan for the stationary rigging assembly is illustrated in Figure 2 on the opposite page.

The erection plan for the traveling rigging assembly is illustrated in Figure 3 on the opposite page.

Figure 4, also shown on the opposite page, illustrates the method of attaching the rope to the swivel eye snap which fastens to the loops on the sides of the belt.

2

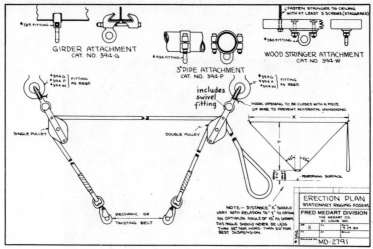

Courtesy of Medart Company,
St. Louis, Missouri.

Figure 2

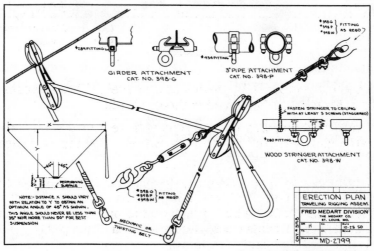

Courtesy of Medart Company,
St. Louis, Missouri.

Figure 3

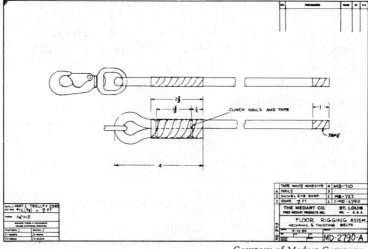

Courtesy of Medart Company,
St. Louis, Missouri.

Figure 4

(a) Overhead Suspension-Belt Spotting—Traveling Rigging

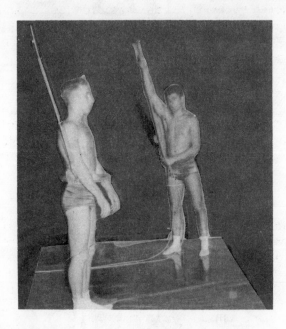

Tumbler stands facing down mat; spotter stands about ten feet down mat at left side. He grasps rope hanging down from overhead suspension with left hand chest high and with right about a foot above his left.

During run forward, spotter keeps ahead of performer and takes up slack on rope with a hand-over-hand action. When spotter reaches take-off spot, he stops. As tumbler turns somersault, spotter pulls rope down below waist with left hand and slides right hand down to left.

If performer is going to land in a faulty manner, spotter can tighten grip on rope with both hands to give added support.

(b) Overhead Suspension-Belt Spotting—Stationary Rigging

With a stationary suspension system, spotter stands at left side of mat at the point of suspension and does not run along mat. Performer can take a short run, but he has to perform stunt directly under suspension point. If performer needs help, spotter can assist in manner described under Overhead Traveling Suspension Rigging.

Spotting is easier with the traveling suspension rigging rather than the stationary. With the former tumbler can take a longer preparatory run and do a greater number of stunts. With the latter, if performer tumbles past suspension point and is supported, he will be pulled back to suspension point. If he has not completed stunt, he may injure himself.

Choosing Stunts

The instructor should teach stunts which are commensurable to the ability of the average student. However, provisions should be made in the instructional program for the skillful student as well as the unskilled student. The skilled may lose interest by performing stunts which are too easy; the unskilled may become discouraged or incur injury by performing stunts which are too difficult.

The instructor can wisely choose the stunts to be included in the program by familiarizing himself with the relative difficulty of many tumbling stunts and with the ability of the members of his classes. In this way he can develop a challenging and varied program.

Class Size

The size of the class has an important bearing on the efficacy of the instruction. A beginning tumbling class should not exceed twenty-five; an advanced class should have less if possible. Capable instructors have effectively taught greater numbers, but this is not an ideal situation. If a class is large, it could be divided in half with one half doing tumbling and balancing; the other half doing activities requiring less supervision.

Student Leaders

Student leaders can assist the instructor in the class arrangement described above. These should be students who have displayed marked skill and leadership ability. These capable youngsters can best be prepared in special sessions at which time their leadership role can be explained to them. Although the instructor cannot leave all the responsibility to student leaders, he must always exercise his trust.

Mats

The minimum requirement of mats for a beginners' group is two mats, twenty feet by five feet by two inches, or four mats, ten feet by five feet by two inches securely tied end to end in a single line without overlapping. If possible two thicknesses of mat should be provided so the tumbler has a softer surface on which to land. These mats should be clean, even in thickness, and free of tears. For advanced groups four twenty-foot mats should be provided of which two are tied securely end to end and placed parallel to the other two also tied end to end about five feet apart and at least fifteen feet from any apparatus or obstructions.

Mats should be placed in position at the start of the class period and removed and carried to a storage area at the end. Class members should do this under the supervision and with the assistance of the class leaders. Mats should be stored flat on a mat truck either in a storage room or in a corner of the gymnasium. If space is unavailable, mats may be hung on hooks protruding from the wall. When stacking mats, to insure that a clean surface will be placed against another clean surface, place them with the top of the first mat up, the top of the second mat against the top of the first, the bottom of the third against the bottom of the second and so forth. Excessively thin mats should be reconditioned or replaced. As soon as torn canvas or plastic covering or loose tuft is noticed, it should be repaired. This care and attention can prolong the life of the mats and eliminate any hazards to the tumbler.

Canvas covered mats in plastic sleeves are more desirable than mats without a plastic sleeve because the former can be kept cleaner easier. However, advanced performers prefer the canvas covered mat without a plastic sleeve because the canvas surface allows a better grip.

The polyethylene foam mat has proven popular because it is resilient and because large sections can be moved easily.

Mats that are used frequently should be sponged off daily with clear water. Excessively dirty mats should be cleaned with detergent or sent back to the manufacturer for cleaning. Canvas surfaces should be vacuumed or swept with a broom.

A sixty feet by five feet by four inch mat in one section is recommended for competitive tumbling. Four inch thickness can be obtained by placing two sixty feet mats on top of one another.

Class Conduct

The class should be divided into squads of ten with one squad assigned to one mat twenty feet long, each student in the squad seated one behind the other facing the mat. This is the best formation for tumbling because the tumblers can tumble down the mat one behind the other at a safe distance and return to their seats by walking off the mats to their left and back on the floor. When observing the class, the instructor should stand about three feet from the mats toward the middle. (See Figure 5 on the following page.)

The best formation for balance work is to have the squads walk down the mats until the first student in each file is two feet from the end of the mat. All then face left, take arms distance with the rear squads dressing behind the first file, and count off by twos. Now they are ready to

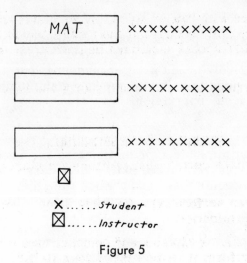

X ...... Student

⊠ ...... Instructor

Figure 5

perform balance stunts, "ones" working first while "twos" assist. Then they reverse their roles. (See Figure 6 below.)

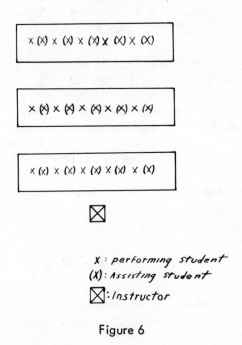

X : performing student

(X): Assisting student

⊠ : Instructor

Figure 6

For doubles balancing, four students should group together with two performing while the other two assist. Then they change.

Each lesson should begin with a review of the previously taught stunts. As these stunts are learned, less and less time should be devoted to them in succeeding lessons. Two new stunts or variations of old ones should be introduced in each lesson if possible. All stunts should be performed in good form, which in tumbling work refers to the ease of performance and the speed and the height of the somersaults. Good form in balance work requires straight arms and legs where indicated, pointed toes and effortless performance.

Costume

For tumbling practice the costume should consist of either a T-shirt or sleeveless shirt, a supporter, either a pair of boxing trunks or a swimming suit, a pair of cotton sox and either

6

low- or high-cut tumbling shoes with rubber soles. A sweatsuit is ideal for warming up. Tennis and basketball shoes are undesirable because of their added weight and because they produce undue wear on the mats. Tumbling barefooted should not be permitted; this practice may contribute to the spread of skin disorders.

Girls should wear leotards or knit shirts and shorts and ballet slippers or gymnastic sandals.

STUDENT'S RESPONSIBILITIES

1. Before attempting a stunt, make certain that spotters are alert and ready to assist if you need their aid.

2. Never change your mind when performing a tumbling stunt. Decide what and how you are going to do it; then do it with determination.

3. Listen attentively while instructor explains and demonstrates a stunt; try to establish a mental picture of the stunt; then perform it to the best of your ability.

4. Learn spotting techniques as conscientiously as tumbling stunts; you may be called on to assist your classmates. Remember their safety depends on the spotter's ability.

5. Do not perform a stunt without assistance until you have tried it many times with assistance.

Chapter   2

Individual Tumbling and Balancing

Whenever possible the stunts and their variations will be presented in a progressing order from the easiest to the most difficult. However, at times, the variations will be more difficult than the original stunt or stunts which follow. The author will indicate when the learning of some stunts should be postponed. For greatest success, practice each stunt until it is mastered under competent instruction and supervision in the order presented. Then proceed to the learning of the next stunt.

After a warm-up, start the workout with the stunts you have learned. Then proceed to new stunts.

Before learning individual tumbling and balancing stunts, perform the following preliminary stunts during the warm-up period. Do the warm-up every time you tumble and workout.

PRELIMINARY STUNTS

(1) Pretzel Bend

Lie down on back with arms either at sides with palms down or overhead with palms up. Rock slowly. This stunt stretches the neck and spinal column, making forward and backward rolling easier.

A

B

A—Raise straight legs upward and above head. Touch mat with toes keeping knees straight. Lower legs slowly to starting position.

B—At first this stunt can be done with bent knees.

(2) Bridge

   (a) Wrestler's Bridge

Lie down on back. Bring legs under body, placing feet on mat with toes turned out.
Lift back off mat, placing top of head on mat. Rock forward and backward.
Lower body to mat.

   (b) High Bridge

Use same procedure as in (2-a), but this time place hands on mat near head with thumbs turned in.

Raise head off mat to support body with hands and feet.

Rise forward to a stand.

(3) Chest Rock

Lie down in a prone position as pictured in picture A of Scale into a Handstand-16j. Instead of placing hands by waist as in starting position of Scale, clasp them behind back.

Lift head, chest and legs off mat.

Rock forward and backward.

The stunts on the following pages are strength exercises which tend to tire and tighten the muscles; therefore, they should be done at the conclusion of the practice and not at the beginning. Do the exercises everyday and when tumbling and balancing seems easier do them every other day.

(1) Push-ups

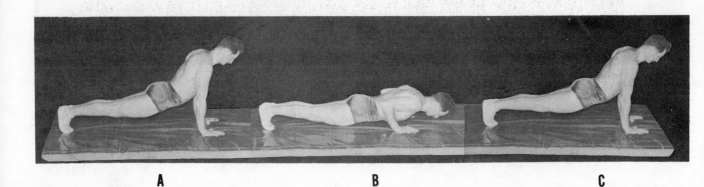

A   B   C

A—Assume a front support.

B—Bend arms to lower body to mat.

C—Straighten arms to raise the straight body off mat. Repeat.

(This exercise develops the arm, back and pectoral muscles.)

When you can do 20 or 30 push-ups, put the feet on a rolled mat so feet are higher than head. When you reach the 30 level do Handstand Push-ups—16i.

(2) Leg Raises

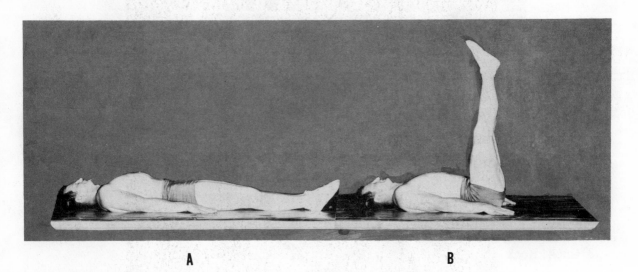

A   B

A—Lie down on back with arms at the sides, palms down.

B—Raise legs almost to a vertical position. Lower slowly to mat. Repeat.

(This exercise develops the lower abdominal and thigh muscles.)

Keep legs straight and together with toes pointed during the raising and lowering.

If your lower back lifts as you raise your legs, spend time doing the Pretzel (preliminary stunt 1). Also, before you start leg raises, pull in the abdominals. This tilts the pelvis back, relieving the pull on the lower back and eliminating back strain from this exercise.

(3) Sit-ups

A   B

A—Lie down on back with arms clasped behind head.

B—Sit up, touching elbows to knees. Repeat slowly.

  (This exercise develops the abdominal muscles.)

Bend the knees and place feet down.   Do bent knee sit-ups.

(4) Deep Knee Bends and Springs

A   B

A—Sit in a deep squat with arms hanging downward and with weight on balls of feet.

B—Spring upward while swinging arms overhead. Land on balls of feet, dropping arms to the sides. Repeat.

  (This exercise develops leg strength, coordination between the spring from the feet and the upward
  lift of the arms and the landing technique. The tumbler should land on balls of feet with knees
  slightly bent in a relaxed manner to absorb the shock of landing.)

11

Stand either on a side horse or bench or table which is supported. Jump off and immediately jump again as high as possible. Repeat many times. This exercise develops spring and is good preparation for the jump Forward Somersault-44; Backward Somersault, Forward Somersault, routine 19; two Forward Somersaults, routine 23; and similar stunts and combinations.

The performer should be able to tumble more easily if he performs the above strength exercises at the conclusion of each workout.

INDIVIDUAL TUMBLING AND BALANCING STUNTS

Introduction

The name which appears first for a particular stunt is one which the author prefers. The other names which follow in parentheses are also used to designate the same stunt.

The series of pictures is spread out for clarity. It may appear the stunt covers a great distance, but in reality it only covers a few feet. The series of pictures of a particular stunt should be viewed many times so a mental picture of the complete performance may be established. To become familiar with them, the description, learning procedure and spotting technique for the stunt should be read carefully many times by the teacher and the performer. Then the teacher is prepared to instruct; the performer is ready to try the stunt with assistance. All stunts with few exceptions should be learned with assistance. Always have two spotters when spotting is indicated.

All the stunts may be done in the direction opposite from that described; however, once a stunt is done to either the right or the left side, all the stunts learned after that must be done in that direction. Girls, however, should do cart wheels in both directions and walkovers on opposite legs because these are often required in compulsory routines.

1. Forward Roll

A B C

A—Take a squat position with legs between arms; place hands flat on mat at shoulders' width with thumbs in and fingers spread.

B—Lift hips, shifting weight from feet to arms. Bend arms, placing back of head on mat. Push off with feet. Roll forward, grasping legs just below knees.

C—Pull onto knees and come to a squat stand. Release grasp and place hands in front on the mat.

(1) Come up in a squat position with knees together and arms raised forward. Do not grasp knees. Do another roll. See first performer in picture above.

(2) Finish in a squat position with one leg ahead of the other. Shift weight from back foot to front and slowly rise to stand bringing arms diagonally upward. Do another Forward Roll from this position of one leg ahead of the other. See second performer in picture above.

(3) From a squat, straddle or piked position roll forward to a sitting position with legs straight and together (piked). Place hands to outside of legs ahead of hips. Lean forward and push up to a piked stand. Do another roll forward. See third performer. If you lack flexibility, this will be difficult to do. Accept the challenge and develop flexibility in the back of the legs.

(4) Roll forward to a sitting position, straddling legs. Place hands between legs and close to thighs. Lean forward, push with hands and rise to a straddled stand. Raise arms forward. Place hands down and do another Forward Roll from the straddled position. See fourth performer above.

2. Backward Roll

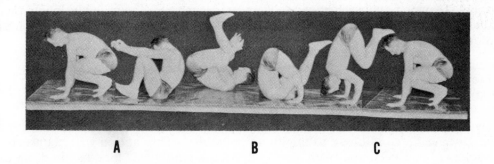

A   B   C

A—Take a squat position. Roll backward with chin on chest.

B—As the back of head touches, place hands flat on mat with thumbs in and fingers spread.

C—Lift shoulders off mat by straightening arms; lift head upward. Complete the roll by placing balls of feet on mat; raise hands off mat.

Learning Procedure

Lie down on back with knees drawn to chest. Roll slowly backward into a Pretzel Bend (preliminary stunt 1). Repeat many times.

This activity should stretch the back and neck muscles enabling the student to perform forward and backward rolls easier.

Spotting Technique

Get the student in a pretzel-bend position with his hands on mat by his head. Stand at the student's back; place hands on either side of student's waist and lift him upward. Do not push him over, since this action might strain his neck muscles. A little lift will enable him to roll over backward, giving him the feel of the stunt.

Methods of Recovery

(1) Roll backward to a Pretzel Bend (preliminary stunt 1). Extend right leg upward and bring left knee to chest. As you push off, place left knee on mat. Raise head and straighten arms, keeping right leg raised as high as possible. This position is called the Knee Scale. Those who are weak in the arms may have to roll over left shoulder, since this requires less strength. As you roll over shoulder, circle head left and around forward.

This is good preparation for the Fishflop-31b.

Recover from kneel by leaning forward and kicking right leg upward. Follow with left leg kick in a scissor action. Reach a momentary Handstand-16. Bring right leg down, keeping left up as high as possible. Keep head up. Push off, straighten up and put left leg down.

Keep legs straight and toes pointed during kick upward and return to mat.

(2) Another variation of this is to land on left foot with right leg raised upward in an Inverted Split, instead of the Knee Scale.

(3) Roll backward with legs straight and together. Extend straight legs backward and apart and push. Land on feet, raise head and straighten arms. Shift weight from arms to legs. Raise straight arms sideward and slightly forward with fingers together. See Straddle-7. Girls may push off, cross arms in front of body and do an outward arm circle, wrists leading. Uncross arms overhead. Turn palms outward and slowly lower them. Place hands on mat close to body. Sit down and do another Backward Roll. See fourth performer in picture under Forward Roll.

(4) Do the same as for the Backward Roll to Straddled Stand above except keep legs together. Raise straight arms overhead.

Recover by lowering arms to sides and bending body forward. Sit down with straight legs, placing chest as close to thighs as possible. This action will counterbalance the sit backward and keep you from sitting down too quickly. Place hands down alongside of thighs and slowly lower hips to mat. Roll backward and perform another Backward Roll.

3. Cartwheel

A

B

A—Stand facing sideward with left leg raised sideward.

B—Lean sideward, placing left hand down in line with left foot, pointing fingers to left.

Kick straight right leg upward, pushing off with left foot. Place right hand down directly in line with left hand, so arms are a shoulders' width apart.

15

C

C—Bring right leg down, placing foot as close to right arm as possible, with toes pointing toward hand. Push off with left hand and then right, straightening up. Pivot on right foot and extend straight arms diagonally upward, holding left leg sideward. Step down on left foot in preparation for a second Cartwheel.

(The head is held up throughout the performance.)

Try to learn two and then a series of Cartwheels without steps between them. Make certain they are performed in a straight line down center of mat.

It should be learned with the right arm leading. This display of ambidexterity is often required in compulsory competitive routines.

16

A   B   C

A—Stand at end of mat, facing forward. Place both hands in center of mat with fingers pointing left sideward. Lift right leg a few inches off mat.

B—Jump around, placing right foot down. Bring left leg behind and beyond right. Momentarily support weight on hands.

C—Push off with left hand and then right; perform a half turn to the left. Place left foot down and bring arms around in front of body. Reach around and place hands down in preparation for another Cartwheel.

This stunt is called a Baby Cartwheel.

Repeat this stunt, kicking the legs higher and higher each time until you finally pass through a Handstand-16.

Spotting Technique

The method of spotting the Cartwheel, Aerial Cartwheel-41, Sideward Somersault-46, all similar stunts in the Cartwheel family, is the same. See spotting method for Sideward Somersault on page 87.

a. One-Handed

Do the One-Handed Cartwheel by placing left hand down only, keeping right out to the side. Kick right leg forcefully and quickly put it down. Left arm and right leg momentarily support the body weight. Now push off with left hand and raise body, putting left leg down. Raise straight arms overhead.

b. Diving Two-Handed

Run forward and do a Hop Step-37. On take-off kick right leg forcefully upward so legs are straddled. Push off with left leg and dive upward. Drop left shoulder and raise right. Throw arms under body, and after a short delay, place hands down as in regular Cartwheel. Bring right leg down and complete stunt.

Spot as for the Aerial Cartwheel and Sideward Somersault-41, 46.

This stunt is excellent preparation for the Aerial Cartwheel.

Put a rolled mat across tumbling mat and have someone sit on one end to keep it from rolling. Do a Diving Cartwheel onto it and then off. This is the same as vaulting over the side horse except it is much lower and performer uses a one-footed take-off.

c. Diving One-Handed

Same as Diving Two-Handed Cartwheel except miss left hand and place right down after a short delay. Continue this until you miss both hands and do an Aerial Cartwheel.

4. Squatstand (Frog Stand)

A   B

A—Get in a squat with legs outside arms. Place hands flat on the mat a shoulders' width apart with thumbs in and fingers spread. Support inside of knees just above elbows.

B—Lean forward, lifting toes off mat. Keep the head up. Do not kick up. Maintain balance by applying pressure with fingers. Return to starting position. Help performer maintain balance by supporting a shoulder and leg.

a. Squat Headstand

Get in a Squatstand. Place head down on mat and hold a balance on head and hands. This is a good preparatory stunt to the Headstand-5.

b. Free

Get in a squat position with legs together. Lean forward and lift feet off mat. Hold with legs unsupported.

c. Dips

Take a Free Squatstand as in 4b. Now bend arms until shoulders almost touch mat. Straighten arms, raising body. Repeat many times.

5. Headstand

a. Kick into a Headstand

A   B   C   (1)

A—Place top of head on mat about six inches ahead of hands which are a shoulders' width apart.

B—Kick the straight right leg overhead into the balance.

C—Bring left leg up to the right, point toes upward. Keep back fairly straight during balance.

18

Methods of Recovery

(1) Lower left leg to mat bending knee; follow with right. Place balls of both feet on mat.

(2) Do a Forward Limberover through Headstand-24a. Later start pushing up to a Handstand-16 and do a Forward Limberover-24.

(3)

(3) Duck head; push off with hands and do a Forward Roll-1 to stand. Come to a stand in the different ways described on page 13 under recovery methods from a Forward Roll.

Spotting Technique

Stand on mat at left side of the performer. As he lifts legs upward, grasp his left thigh with hands; support and balance him; slowly release the hold on his thigh, keeping hands a few inches from his leg. See the Spotting Technique for 16 a Handstand. Employ the same technique for spotting the Headstand.

b. Squat Press into Headstand

A   B   C   (1)

A—Get in a squat position with legs between arms as in picture A preceding. The Headstand may also be done from a Squatstand-4 as in first picture of second series following.

B—Lean forward, placing top of head on mat about six inches ahead of hands. Do not move head or hands once they are in position.

C—Raise and extend legs overhead, pointing toes upward.

D—Arch back.

Methods of Recovery

Use same recovery methods as for Kick into Headstand.

c. Straight Leg Press into Headstand (Piked Press)

A   B   C   (1)

A—Place head down about six inches ahead of hands which are a shoulders' width apart. Bend at hips with legs straight and together and toes touching mat (piked position).

B —Raise straight legs overhead into Headstand.

C—Keep back fairly straight.

     Keep toes pointed.

As an exercise do the piked press into a Headstand and lower over and over without pause.

Methods of Recovery

Lower straight legs slowly to mat.

Employ the other recovery methods mentioned for Kick into a Headstand-5a.

6. Split

Extend left leg forward and right backward. Keep both legs straight throughout slide downward. Touch sole of left foot and instep of right foot to floor. Do not sit on right hip. Support body weight on legs.

Change legs so right leg is forward and left backward as pictured above.

Learning Procedure

Slowly extend legs into split, but before you reach floor with legs place hands down on either side to ease strain of stretch. As you attain greater flexibility, hold arms sideward and push legs slowly to floor.

Methods of Recovery

(1) Roll slightly to left hip, bend left knee and kneel on it. Step forward on right foot and rise to a stand.

(2) With arms sideward, pull backward, sliding left heel on floor. Shift weight over right leg and kneel on right knee.

(3) Place right hand down to right opposite left thigh. Roll right over right leg. Bring left leg around, placing left foot down with knee bent. Place left hand down by left thigh and bring right arm across chest. Turn left, rolling over bent left leg. Land on left knee with right leg extended backward. Bring right leg forward and put right foot down, shifting weight from left knee to right foot.

This recovery amounts to a sideward roll through a split.

(4) Bend forward over left leg and grasp left ankle with both hands. Roll right sideward, maintaining hold of left leg. Release left leg. Bring legs down forward in a split. Place right foot down with knee bent and extend left leg forward. See middle performer in picture on the following page.

(5) Draw legs together and rise to a stand with or without use of hands. This method is the opposite of going down into a split. This recovery takes a great deal of leg strength.

(6) Turn right sideward into a Straddle-7, and do a Forward Roll-1.

Flexibility can only be attained through daily work over a long period of time. If the person is inherently flexible, some time should be spent maintaining this flexibility, but most should be devoted to strength skills and exercises. The individual with taut ligaments and tendons should spend most of his time stretching.

7. Straddle

Extend both legs sideward. Continue extension until inner side of legs and soles of feet touch floor. Solo performer is higher off mat than described previously.

Lean forward and place chest and arms on mat. Sit back as you lean forward.

This is called a Japanese Split, but is actually a Straddle. See performer on right of trio pictured above.

Learning Procedure

Use same learning procedure as for Split-6, but this time place hands in front instead of to the sides.

Methods of Recovery

(1) Place both hands down in front of legs. Draw legs together in the back, squat up or pike up. Rise to a stand.

(2) Draw legs together slowly, rising to a stand without use of arms.

The Split-6 and Straddle-7 can be done anywhere in the progression. They should be used as part of the warm-up program which includes the Pretzel Bend and High Bridge (preliminary stunts 1 and 2).

22

Once a good Straddle is learned it can be incorporated into a Straddle Jump as pictured below.

The Straddle Jump and other Jumps into a Handstand-16 and Forward Somersault-44 are described under the Learning Procedure for the Backward Somersault, Forward Somersault, routine 19 on page 183. These Jumps and dives into Handstands can be learned any time after a good Handstand is learned.

The poses pictured below and on the following page can be used in the Floor Exercise Event. These stunts like the Split-6 and Straddle-7 can be introduced anywhere in the progression. They are simple stunts to try, but to do well require a great deal of practice.

A

B

C

D

8. Arabesque (leg in attitude position)

This is shown by first performer on left in picture A, page 23. Straddle flexibility is needed if performer is to lift right leg into the attitude position.

9. Front Scale

Middle girl performer is shown in Scale with arms back in picture A, page 23. Boy performer has his arms sideward. He shows exceptional flexibility in the split position.

10. Single Leg Stand (leg in front attitude position)

This is shown by performer on right in picture A, page 23.

11. Single Leg Stand (leg raised sideward)

This is shown by performer on left in picture C, above. She grasps her left heel with her left hand and raises her left leg sideward to a straddled position.

12. Swedish Fall

Performer falls to a prone position with straight right leg raised as high as possible. In the case of performer shown on right side her left leg is raised, picture C above. On landing she bends arms and carefully lowers chest to mat, holding leg high.

13. V Support

Performer leans back slightly and lifts legs and hips off (picture D above).

Learning Procedure

Do a V sit with arms raised sideward many times.
Do an L support many times. It is first picture of 16n.

14. Forearm-Headstand (Elbow-Headstand)

A   B   C

A—Place forearms down with thumbs and index fingers touching. Extend right leg backward and keep left bent up close to chest. Place top of head in space formed by thumbs and index fingers.

(The hands may be clasped and placed behind head during the balance instead of as described above.)

B—Kick straight right leg upward and overhead into balance.

C—Bring left leg up to right.

Performer can get into balance by kicking or pressing up with his legs in either a squat or piked position. See Headstand-5.

Use recovery methods described for Headstand.

Spotting Technique

The spotting technique is the same as for the Headstand-5 and the Handstand-16. This technique is used for practically all balance stunts that warrant assistance.

15. Forearmstand (Elbowstand)

A   B   C

The techniques for performing the Forearmstand are the same as for the Forearm-Headstand-14 except that the head is raised off mat.

The recovery methods are the same as those described for Headstand-5.

Spotting Technique

The spotting technique is the same as for the Headstand-5 and the Handstand-16a.

16. Handstand

a. Kick into Handstand

A—Raise straight arms and left leg forward.

B—Bend forward and place left foot down.

C—Keep left leg straight and kick straight right leg upward.

D—Rise to Handstand and bring right leg to left. Keep arms straight, legs straight and together, toes pointed and back straight. Description is opposite to that pictured above.

Methods of Recovery

(1) (a) Lower left straight leg to mat, keeping straight right leg up as high as possible. Slowly lift arms off. Raise upper body and head and bring arms sideward into a Front Scale-9.

(b) Lower as (1), (a), above, except keep hands down and hold an Inverted Split (right leg straight up and left straight down) if you are flexible enough.

(c) Lower right leg to mat and push off with hands. Do a half turn left on right foot. Swing both arms sideward, ending with them out to the sides or swing them upward parallel to each other, keeping them overhead during body rotation. Lower arms down and to side. Keep left leg horizontal to ground during and after rotation.

Either the right or left leg can be lowered to mat; however, when right is placed down, performer can turn in his natural direction to the left. Then he can do a Cartwheel-3, Roundoff-19, or Forward Handspring-38 with left foot and hand leading. If he places his left foot down first and turns to the right, he cannot lead with his left foot. However, he can solve this by doing a Switch Kick Forward Walkover-26a. He steps on his right foot and kicks his left upward, opposite of what he normally does. As left leg reaches vertical, he raises his right leg to vertical, quickly lowering his left to the horizontal. While in this position, he continues his forward movement and does the Forward Walkover, landing, as he does naturally, on his right foot first.

(2) Instead of lowering left leg to mat bring it between arms and lower to a Split-6. When you lower legs, lean shoulders forward so body is under control. Keep legs straight.

Bringing the leg through is easier if performer can do a Handstand on his fingers.

(3) (a) Bring legs down, straight and together with toes pointed. Place feet as close to hands as possible into a Piked position. Raise upper body.

(b) Bring legs down between arms to an L support-16n, A, or V support-13.

(4) (a) Straddle legs as wide as possible and bring them down to a Straddled Stand-7.

(b) Bring legs down, straddled beyond hands. Support legs on thighs.

(5) Limberover-24 or Walkover-26 to a stand.

(6) Forward Roll out with body in a Piked position with arms bent or with arms straight. Rise to a stand in the several ways described under Forward Roll recovery methods.

(7) From a Handstand with legs split, left forward and right back, lean and fall left sideward, supporting weight on left arm. Drop into a Split-6 with left leg forward and right back. Push off with left hand and raise arms sideward and upward.

Performer does Cartwheel to Handstand with legs together. As she falls left sideward, she places right leg forward and left back opposite of that described above.

Spotting Technique

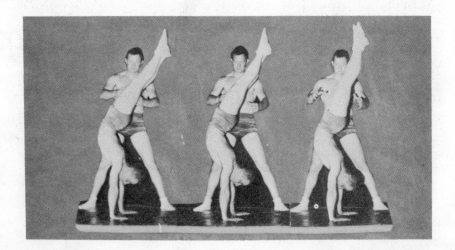

The spotting technique used for the Handstand is the same as for the Headstand-5. This technique is used for practically all balances. Use it in helping the performer do 16b and 16c.

Learning Procedure
Handstand against the wall

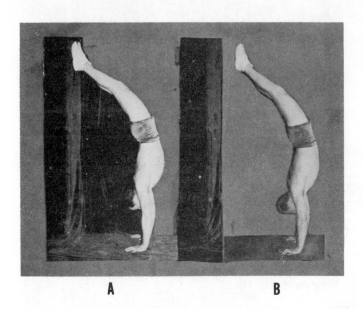

A B

A—Place the hands on mat about eighteen inches from the wall. Kick up slowly through a Handstand, bringing feet to rest against the wall.

B—Slowly push away with toes and at the point of balance, stiffen the body and limbs in an attempt to hold the balance. Hold the Handstand as long as possible; then return to the wall. When tired, return to a stand.

Fight overbalance by raising the head high, overarching the back and pressing hard on the fingertips.

Fight underbalance by bending the arms and by pushing the shoulders forward.

b. Headstand into a Handstand

(1) Kick into Handstand

A B C D

A—Perform a Headstand-5.

B—Bend knees.

C—Then extend them forcefully upward, rising into a Handstand.

D—At the time of the kick, straighten arms and lift head upward.

(2) Press into Handstand

A   B

A—Straighten arms and underbalance Handstand slightly.

B—Slowly bring body back into balance.

Learning Procedure

(1) Use the same procedure as for the Handstand against the wall-16a.

(2) Place head on top of several mats and hands on the floor. Then perform a Headstand-5. (With head raised about four inches, it is easier to press into Handstand.) Press into a Handstand.

Spotting Technique

Use the same technique as for the Headstand-5 and Handstand-16a.

c. Handstand Walks

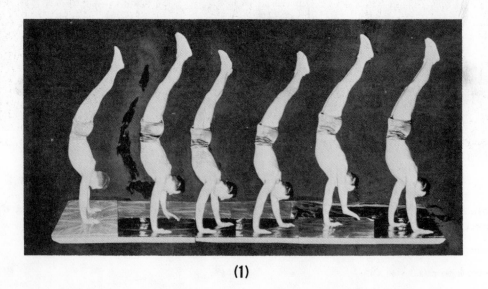

(1)

Do not walk until you have perfected a stationary Handstand.

(1) Forward

Overbalance Handstand slightly. Lean right and place left hand about six inches directly ahead. Lean left and move right hand about the same distance ahead. Repeat.

(2) Backward

Underbalance Handstand slightly. Lean right and place left hand about six inches directly back. Lean left and move right hand about the same distance back. Repeat.

(3) Sideward

Lean left sideward and raise right arm off mat. Place it within a shoulders' width of left arm. Slide left hand left sideward a few inches. Move right arm again toward left. Continue moving sideward.

Spotting Technique

Same as for Headstand-5 and Handstand.

d. Squat Press into Handstand (Bent Arm, Bent Leg Press) (Tuck Press)

Handstand may also be pressed from Squatstand-4 or from a squat position. The former is easier to master and is similar in technique to the press from a squat position pictured below.

A   B   C   D   E

A—Take a squat position with legs between arms. Place hands flat on mat with thumbs in and fingers spread.

B—Lean forward bending arms. Raise bent legs together off mat.

C—Raise hips overhead slowly.

D—Straighten arms and legs and bring shoulders back over hands.

E—Point toes upward and stretch to avoid overarching.

31

e. Straddled Press into a Handstand (Bent Arm, Straight Leg Straddled Press)

A   B   C

A—Get into a straddled position. Lean forward placing hands on mat in front of legs. Lean farther forward bending arms.

B—Raise the straight straddled legs off mat with hips upward.

C—Raise legs overhead and straighten hips.

Slowly bring legs together.

f. Piked Press into Handstand (Bent Arm, Straight Leg Piked Press)

Use the same procedure in doing this stunt as in the straddled press into a Handstand-16e above, but this time keep legs together.

g. Straight Arm, Squat Press into Handstand (Straight Arm, Bent Leg Press)

This stunt is done the same as Squat Press into a Handstand-16d with the exception that arms are kept straight. Lean forward during the press.

32

Place the left hand on performer's left shoulder and right hand on his hip for support. Have performer press into handstand and slowly return to starting position. Repeat. Follow performer's movement with hands. Use two spotters.

h. Piked Press into Handstand (Straight Arm, Straight Leg Press)

This stunt is the same as Bent Arm, Straight Leg Piked Press into Handstand-16f except arms are kept straight. Lean forward during press and lift hips overhead. As you bring legs overhead, bring shoulders back over hands. Do not overarch Handstand.

Spotting Technique

Use the same technique as for the Bent Arm, Straight Leg Piked Press into a Handstand-16g.

i. Handstand Push-ups

A   B   C

A—Perform a Handstand.

B—Bend arms and slowly lower body so shoulders are forward and face is a few inches from the mat. Maintain the balance.

C—Return to Handstand by straightening arms and bringing the shoulders back over hands. Repeat.

33

j. Scale into Handstand (Arched Press into Handstand) (Hollow Back Press)

A   B   C

A—Lie down in a prone position with head up and hands on mat next to hip bones.

B—Lift body a few inches off mat into a Planche with bent arms.

C—Press into the Handstand by bringing shoulders back over hands and straightening arms.

k. Chestroll into Handstand

A   B   C

A—Roll forward hitting chest and hands simultaneously. Hold head back.

B—Push upward raising body off mat.

C—Continue push into Handstand without losing momentum from roll.

This stunt when performed slowly can be used as the Learning Procedure for the Scale into a Handstand—16j.

(The Chestroll may be done into the Headstand—5.)

1. Fallout, Straddle to Handstand

A

B

C

D

E   F

G   H

Lean shoulders forward and overbalance Handstand. Fall with straight arms. Place back of head on mat and roll forward. At a straddle V sit position, place hands close to body. Shift shoulders forward, lowering straight legs. Lift hips up and draw legs back. Keeping legs close to body, lift hips overhead. Straighten hips into Handstand with legs straddled. Bring straight legs together with toes pointed.

m. Split, Press to Handstand

Lean forward in Split-6 and start lifting hips upward and drawing legs together. As legs pull out from in front of arms, lift hips into Handstand. Straighten hips.

n. L, Press to Handstand

A

B

C

D

E

F

From L position pull hips back and shift shoulders a little ahead of hands. Continue press by lifting hips to horizontal and shifting shoulders forward a little more. Raise hips without leaning any farther. Keep legs close to chest in a tightly piked position. Lift feet up and slide legs back behind hands. Straddle legs and bring hips overhead. Extend hips into Handstand. Hold and slowly bring legs together. Performer is on fingertips.

o. Jumps

A   B   C

A—Perform Handstand. Overbalance it slightly.

B—Quickly bend arms and legs.

C—Then forcefully extend them and spring off performing a jump forward.

Repeat these jumps in a rapid fashion down mat.

p. With One Arm

A B C

A—Perform Handstand.

B—Stretch body upward and lean to left rising up on fingertips of right hand. Lock left shoulder and arm.

C—When you get balance, slowly lift fingers off and then raise arm sideward.

(Start on this stunt when you have perfected a two-arm Handstand.)

The picture above shows how one arm Handstand may be done on a pedestal or on other apparatus. The one armer can be performed easier on apparatus than on the floor.

q. Forearm Press into a Handstand (Tiger Bend Press)

Perform a Forearmstand-15.

Overbalance the stunt. Push shoulders forward and quickly lift forearms off mat. This sudden lift will result in an underbalance. Slowly raise body over hands and extend arms.

r. Yogi Handstand

Do a Handstand.

Pike at hips.

Lift head up and lock shoulders.

If the performer has difficulty doing Handstand variations, he should practice the stunts which follow and return to them later.

17. Jump with a Twist

a. Half Twist

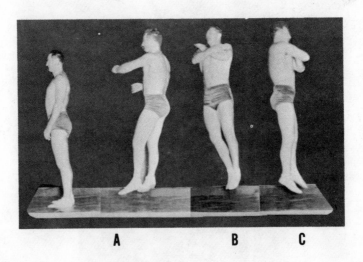

A—Jump forward and raise bent arms forward in front of chest.

B—Throw right arm across chest and left arm backward.

C—At the same time, turn head and body sharply to left, performing the Half Twist.

(Try twisting in both directions to determine which is easier.)

b. Full Twist (360 degree turn)

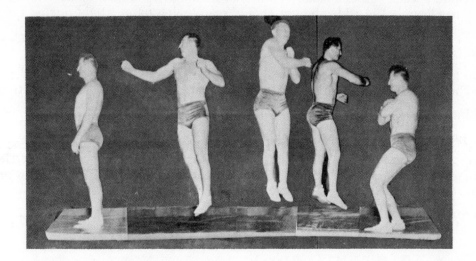

Jump upward as high as possible without leaning to either side. Twist as described on the opposite page for the Half Twist, but throw arms, head and body more forcefully in the direction of twist.

c. Full and Half Twist (One and Half Twist)

d. Double Twist

Both the One and a Half and Double Twists are done the same as the Full with the exception that the greater twists are done with more force. Remember to jump straight upward before the twist.

18. Snapdown from a Momentary Handstand

A   B   C   D   E

A—Kick into a momentary Handstand—16a.

B—Slowly underbalance the handstand and bend knees.

C—Then forcefully extend legs backward and push off with hands.

D—Bend at hips, bringing bent knees under body. (There should be a period of momentary flight before landing.)

E—Land on balls of feet and raise arms overhead.

41

Learning Procedure

Roll up a ten-foot mat. Place hands on mat and kick up into a momentary Handstand-16a. Perform a Snapdown. The added height should enable you to get flight during the kick downward. Decrease height of mat until you can perform stunt from a flat mat.

a. With Half Twist

Perform a Snapdown. Just before landing, twist right hip inward and throw right arm across chest. Twist left and land with knees bent, facing in opposite direction.

See Backward Handspring with Half Twist-routine 9.

b. Donkey Jumps (Continuous Snapdowns)

Kick into a Handstand-16a. Perform Snapdown, landing on balls of feet a little off balance with knees bent and arms raised forward. Spring off both feet into a Handstand, diving close to feet. Perform another Snapdown. Continue this sequence rapidly many times.

(If done properly, this stunt is funny.)

19. Roundoff

A   B   C   D   E

A—Perform Hop Step-37. Lean forward, deeply bending left knee. Swing left arm in front of body.

B—Place left hand down a little to right of center of mat with fingers pointing backward toward feet.

C—Kick straight right leg backward and upward and push off with left foot. Do a half turn left (counterclockwise) into a momentary one-handed Handstand-16p with left shoulder and body stretched. To do a straight Roundoff, you must pass through a Handstand with body straight.

D—Place right hand on opposite side of center of mat about 12 inches back. Both hands should be turned in same direction.

E—Immediately perform a Snapdown-18, ending with arms raised forward.

The Roundoff is one of the most important individual tumbling stunts. With it the performer can turn himself halfway around and continue tumbling down the mat in the direction of the run without losing any momentum.

The Barani-43, and the Forward Somersault with a Half Twist-44c are the only other stunts besides the Roundoff which can be used for this purpose.

When performer kicks right leg, he must extend it backward. This will extend his left shoulder, making a straight line from his left hand to his feet and assuring him of a straight turn around his longitudinal axis.

If he ends up facing slightly left at end of Roundoff (overtwisted), he has either forced his shoulder out to left side or placed left hand down too far right of center at start or he has brought right arm around too far while completing half turn.

If he ends up facing slightly right at the end (undertwisted), he has placed his left hand down to left of center at start.

If either of these faults persist, performer should start over with Learning Procedure (1).

A crooked Roundoff will cause stunts which follow to go crooked, a serious problem which must be rectified as soon as possible.

If you are preparing to do a Backward Handspring from Roundoff, land with knees bent and arms extended forward (see picture A, page 164). Do not spring off mat.

If preparing for a Backward Somersault from Roundoff, spring, raising straight arms upward. (See picture under Learning Procedure for Roundoff, Backward Somersault, page 166.)

Learning Procedure

A   B   C   D

(1) A—Stand on floor at right side of mat. Then turn forty-five degrees to left. Place left foot on edge of mat diagonally forward.

   B—Bend left leg, placing left hand about a foot diagonally ahead with fingers pointing backward.

   C—Kick straight right leg upward and push off with left foot, executing a three-eighths turn counter-clockwise (to left) into a momentary one-handed Handstand-16p.

   D—Place right hand on opposite side of center of mat about a foot back. Perform a Snapdown-18.

(2) Face down mat with left foot leading. Kick into Cartwheel-3. As you reach Handstand-16, turn body one-fourth turn left and bring legs together. Do a Snapdown-18. Do this many times, gradually turning hands around until fingers point backward. As you turn hands, place left to right of center and right to left of center.

After properly learning these steps, you are ready to perform a Roundoff as described previously from a stand with feet on either side of center line of mat.

a. With One Hand

   Do a one-handed Roundoff same as two-handed except place left hand in center of mat instead of to one side. Hold right arm sideward.

   If performer is going crooked on a two-handed Roundoff by trying a one-handed he may discover and correct his faults.

b. Diving Two-Handed

Take off from one foot with arms raised. Spring upward, throwing arms downward toward feet. Twist body a half turn. Land on hands and do Snapdown-18.

c. Diving One-Handed

Same as two-handed except right hand is placed down only. Keep doing this until you miss right hand also, doing an Aerial Roundoff.

Stunts 19b and 19c are excellent lead-ups to the Barani-43.

20. Butterfly

A—Stand in center of mat, facing to one side. Swing arms and twist body to right. Shift weight over right leg.

B—Bend forward and swing arms left sideward in front of legs, shifting weight to left foot.

C—Kick right leg as high as possible.

D—Push off with left foot.

E—Keep head up, but lower than legs. Continue arm swing, completing one-half turn. Bring right straight leg down and raise left.

F—Land on right foot with toes turned to right. Then pivot on right foot so it is turned sideward. Put left foot down with toes turned left. Finish arm swing in front of body.

Learning Procedure

Do a leaping half turn with body upright. This turn is similar to the Butterfly turn except it is done on a vertical plane while the Butterfly turn is done on a horizontal plane. Continue lowering body during succeeding turns until you perform a Butterfly.

Spotting Technique

Stand facing performer. Grasp his hands with your palms up and his down. Pull performer around sideward, simulating the Butterfly. Now you have changed positions. If performer is same size as spotter, he can take role of spotter and spin his partner around. This can be a nice doubles tumbling stunt if done continuously.

21. Diving Forward Roll

A   B   C   D   E   F   G

a. From Standing Position

A—Lean forward.

B—Swing the arms downward and backward, rising on the toes.

C—Swing the arms forward, straightening the knees. Spring off balls of feet, diving forward.

D—Land with arms straight, absorbing shock of landing; duck head and bend arms, placing back of head on mat.

E—Round back and roll forward.

F—Grasp legs just below knees.

G—Pull legs under body and rise to a stand.

Learning Procedure

(1) Lean forward until the hands are a few inches off the mat. Spring off performing a Forward Roll-1.

(2) Spring higher and higher until you perform a high-diving Forward Roll from a stand.

(Do not omit any steps in this learning procedure.)

b. From Run

The dive is preceded by a run and a Hurdle-22. The run enables the performer to dive higher and longer. Do not attempt a running dive until you have mastered the dive from a standing position.

22. Hurdle (from a run)

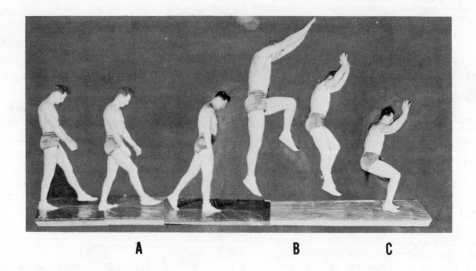

A—End run on right foot.

B—Raise arms and bent left leg upward. Spring upward off right foot.

C—Land on balls of both feet with knees bent slightly, leaning slightly forward. Keep arms raised overhead.

The Hurdle precedes the Diving Forward Roll-21 from a run as well as the Forward Somersault-44.

The stunts which follow, the Backbend and its variation, the Limbers, Chestrolls, Splits, Straddles, and Walkovers are all acrobatic stunts. They all have a purpose in a boy's and girl's tumbling program; however, acrobatic work solely without fast tumbling is not desirable from a gymnastic standpoint. The overflexibility developed in acrobatic work is a detriment to the performer, boy or girl, who wants to excel in the other gymnastic events of Floor Exercise, Vaulting, and Apparatus work.

Acrobatic performers work slowly and with great flexibility but usually lack strength and power. They are also called contortionists.

Ideal tumblers are those who have flexible and strong backs, arms, legs, and shoulders. Because of their strength and power, they can tumble fast and high and can also perform acrobatic movements when necessary in Floor Exercise and on the Apparatus.

23. Backbend

A   B   C

a. From Stand

A—Stand with arms overhead and head back.

B—Lower backward, stretching arms and thrusting hips forward. Do not bend at hips, do not bend knees if possible and keep heels down on mat.

C—Drop gently to mat, placing hands flat with thumbs pointing inward as close to feet as possible with knees almost straight. Hold a high arch. Rise to stand by thrusting hips forward and pushing off with hands.

Learning Procedures

(1) Learn well a High Bridge-2b and return to a stand before lowering to a Backbend from a stand.

(2) Stand about a foot from a rolled mat and lower to this mat. Do this many times rising to a stand each time. Then while standing on one mat, lower to a pile of three mats. Finally, do it on one level surface.

Spotting Techniques

(1) Place hands on performer's lower back and back of knee as if spotting the Backward Handspring-40. Support performer enough so he does not crash down while lowering. Push performer forward as he rises to a stand. As his proficiency improves, support less and less. This is true in all spotting: as performer improves give less and less assistance.

(2) Stand facing performer and place one leg between his legs. Grasp him across lower back. Pull him toward you as he lowers backward. As his hands touch, release hold. To help performer rise to stand, pull him toward you as he pushes off. Help as much as needed.

b. With One Leg Raised

Raise right leg to the vertical. Hold. Lower and raise left leg. Hold. Then lower. Keep knee straight when leg is raised.

c. Prancing Horse

Same as preceding except as you lower one leg raise other leg. Continue this alternately kicking legs, simulating the action of a prancing horse. Eventually performer will kick left leg hard enough to pass through a Handstand and do a Backward Walkover-25.

d. With One Hand

Same as preceding, but this time hold only the right arm overhead. After lowering the body, place hand on mat. Hold left arm out to the side. Rise to a stand.

e. Walk Backward (Crab Walk)

Lower into Backbend. Walk by moving right and then left hand ahead. Move right and left feet alternately toward hands. As at the start, body is in a high arch again. Continue walking in manner described above.

f. Inside-Out Turns

Lower into Backbend.

Reach upward and across chest with right arm, twisting body. Push off with right foot, completing body turn. End in a piked position.

Continue turn by lifting left leg across right. Push off with left hand completing turn into Backbend. Repeat.

(This stunt can be done rapidly and with a bouncing motion.)

Picture shows opposite of description.

g. Without Hands

Do this stunt the same as Backbend, but this time hold arms sideward and thrust hips farther forward to control the lowering of the body. Turn feet straight out to side and as you lower, roll onto inside of feet. Touch head to mat. To rise thrust hips forward forcefully.

24. Forward Limberover (Forward Bridgeover)

A   B   C

A—Kick up and through a momentary Handstand–16.

B—Stretch shoulders, back and hips, lowering legs so feet touch within two and a half feet of hands with toes turned out and arms straight.

C—Thrust hips forward and push off with hands, stretching shoulders and hips. Rise to a stand with arms overhead. Do not bend at hips.

Keep head back and body arched, but not excessively. Perform stunt slowly.

Spotting Technique

Place right hand on small of back and left hand either on shoulder or on upper arm.

Use two spotters.

49

a. Through Headstand

This is the same as the Limberover-24 except you pass through a Headstand-5 instead of a Handstand-16.

The spotting technique is the same as for the Limberover-24; however, if spotters kneel, it would be easier for them to lift performer.

It is better if performer learns a Limberover rather than a Headstand Bridgeover. From the latter he may develop a habit of bending his arms on the Limberover. The Headstand Bridgeover is a good stunt for those who lack back flexibility.

b. With One Hand (Forward Limberover One-Handed)

This is the same as the Limberover except only one hand is placed down. Place right hand in center of mat and hold left out to the side.

Use the same spotting technique as for the other Bridgeovers.

25. Backward Walkover

A

B

C

D

A—Stand with arms overhead and left leg forward with weight on right foot.

B—Rock backward and push off with right foot.

C—Rise into a momentary Handstand-16, with legs straight in Split-6, left leg leading.

D—Lower straight left leg to mat and push off with hands.

E—Rise to a stand, lowering right leg.

Pictures show opposite leg leading.

E

Spotting Technique

Kneel on right knee at left side of performer with left leg extended sideward. As he bends backward, place right hand on his back and left hand on back of thigh. Support performer with hand on back and help him over by lifting his left leg with left hand.

Recovery Methods

The split Handstand must be controlled the same as the Handstand with legs together, before performer can lower his legs into the various recovery methods.

(1) From split Handstand lower straight left leg, keeping right leg vertical if possible to a split stand. Hands can remain on the mat or arms can be raised sideward; however, split stand must be maintained as arms are raised. (See Recovery Methods 1a and 1b from Handstand, page 27.)

(2) While passing through the split Handstand, switch legs so right leg is leading and left is back (Switchkick Back Walkover). This is the same as the Switchkick Forward Walkover except direction is reversed. Step down on straight right leg and do a half turn left. (See Recovery Method 1c from Handstand, page 27.)

(3) From split Handstand lower straight left leg between arms to a Split-6. (See Recovery Method 2 from Handstand, page 27.)

As left leg is lowered, lean left and cut left leg across right arm to a Split. This is easier than bringing it between arms.

(4) From split Handstand lower left leg to right so both are horizontal. Shift shoulders forward so piked position can be held momentarily and legs can be lowered in a controlled manner. Rise to an erect stand. (See Recovery Method 3a from Handstand, page 27.)

(5) Same as (4) above, except pike legs through to an L or V support. (See Recovery Method 3b from Handstand, page 27.)

(6) From a split Handstand rotate hips so legs are straddled. Lower to a Straddled Stand-7, page 22. (See Recovery Method 4a, page 27.)

(7) Same as (6), except bring legs through and rest inside of thighs on arms in a Straddled support. (See Recovery Method 4b, page 27.) Pull legs back and press up to a Handstand, the second half of 1, page 27.

(8) From a split Handstand lean and fall left sideward, supporting weight on left arm. Drop into a Split-6 with left leg forward and right backward. Push off with left hand and raise arms sideward. (See Recovery Method 7 and also pictures on page 28.)

a. With One Hand

Bend backward, placing right hand in center of mat. Do a Backward Walkover with the left arm sideward.

51

b. Spotters

Do a Backward Walkover. Take a normal stride forward with right foot. Swing left leg forward, and raise arms overhead. Perform another Backward Walkover. Continue Walkovers staying on same spot.

26. Forward Walkover

A   B   C

A—Raise arms upward and straight left leg forward. Step down and kick through a Handstand with legs in a split position right leg forward.

B—Lower straight legs with right leg leading. Bring right foot down in center of mat as close to hands as possible, keeping right hip extended.

C—Push off with hands and rise to a stand with left leg raised forward. Lower it, keeping arms raised overhead.

The spotting technique is the same as for the Forward Limberover-24.

a. Switchkick

Lead off with right foot forward instead of left. Kick left leg upward and push off with right. As left reaches vertical, stop it. Bring right to vertical as you bring left back to horizontal. With legs split continue through Handstand-16, landing on right foot first.

b. With One Hand

Perform one-handed Walkover like two-handed, but this time place right hand in center of mat while holding left arm sideward.

c. Spotters

Do a Forward Walkover, landing on right foot with left raised. Instead of placing left foot down, step back a normal stride with it. Bend forward, swinging right leg backward. Place hands close to left foot and do another Walkover. Continue Walkovers, remaining on the same spot.

d. Diving

Dive upward not forward, bringing arms down toward take-off spot. Land on hands, and slowly do a Walkover.

e. Diving One-Handed

Same as above except with one hand. Do not dive forward. Spot it.

   (1) Land on right foot; step forward on left and slide forward into a Split-6.

   (2) Instead of landing on right foot, land on front of right foot and fall controlled to left foot into a high split position. Slide forward on left the rest of the way down.

27. Backward Limberover

A

B

C

C

A—Do a Backbend-23.

B—Rock backward, kicking both legs overhead so body passes through a momentary Handstand-16a. Get legs together as soon as possible after pushoff.

C—Lower both legs to mat. Push off with hands, and rise to a stand with arms overhead.

Performer should be discouraged from doing this as a preparation for a Backward Handspring-40. He may develop a bad habit of not springing for Handspring.

If performer does not have the flexibility needed to perform stunts, 23 through 30, he should leave them and try the stunts which follow. When his flexibility increases, he should return to these stunts.

28. Valdez

A

B

C

D

D

A—Sit with left leg extended and right bent. Place right hand down with thumb out and raise straight left arm forward.

B—Throw left arm overhead and kick straight left leg upward. Push off with right, straightening it and stretching right hip.

C—Place left hand down with thumb in and pass through a split Handstand.

D—Pivot on right hand, turning thumb in. Bring straight left leg down, then right.

Do not push up to a High Bridge-preliminary stunt 2b. Instead pass continuously through a Handstand like a Backward Walkover by throwing left arm and pushing off with right foot.

Spotting Technique

Kneel at left side of performer. Place right hand on lower back and left behind left knee, the same as for Backward Handspring-40. Do this to support unsupported left side. As performer throws, lift her through Backward Walkover-25.

55

29. Forward Chestroll

A B C D E F

A—Start in a standing position with hands at sides of chest. Lean backward arching back.

B —Rock forward, keeping arch.

C—Let thighs hit.

D—Continue roll to chest.

E —Turn head to right and push off with hands, lifting body off mat. Continue roll until feet touch mat.

F —Push upward with hands and rise to a stand with arms raised.

Learning Procedure

(1) Perform a Chest Rock preliminary stunt-3, using the hands to push. Try to get the legs overhead on the rock forward.

(2) Now do the Chestroll from a kneeling position. After you learn this, do the Chestroll from a stand.

Spotting Technique

Stand at right side of performer and place both hands on performer's right thigh as performer gets into a cheststand position. Lift upward to facilitate the performer's roll. This technique is similar to spotting Backward Roll into Headstand-31. The object in spotting this stunt is to take pressure off performer's neck when he is on face in a vertical position. This is accomplished by lifting the performer upward when he reaches this position.

Girls can do Chestrolls better than boys because generally they have greater body flexibility. Boys are more successful at Chestrolls to a Headstand or Handstand because these stunts require greater arm strength.

a. Cheststand

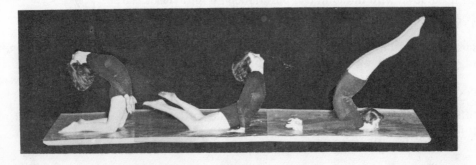

From a kneeling position with arms at sides and thumbs out, roll forward to chest with legs overhead. Hold balance by applying pressure with hands.

Recovery Method

Bend arms and place hands by shoulders with thumbs turned in. With straight body, press to a Handstand-16.

b. Forward Chestrolls Grasping Ankles (Snake Rolls)

From a stand, do a Backbend-23 and grasp ankles. Thrust hips forward and turn feet outward. Then roll forward over knees, thighs, front of body and left side of face.

Pull feet over and place them by head. Thrust hips forward again and rise to a stand.

Start another roll or release hold on ankles. Then straighten body.

Learning Procedure

Perform a snake roll from a kneeling start. After learning it properly, try the roll from a stand.

30. Backward Chestroll

A—Raise arms overhead.

B —Perform a Backbend-23, placing hands as close to feet as possible.

C—Bend arms and place left side of face on mat.

D—Push off with feet.

E —Roll backward over front of body.

F —Push off with hands.

G—Rise to a stand with back arched. Perform another roll or straighten body.

31. Backward Roll into Headstand

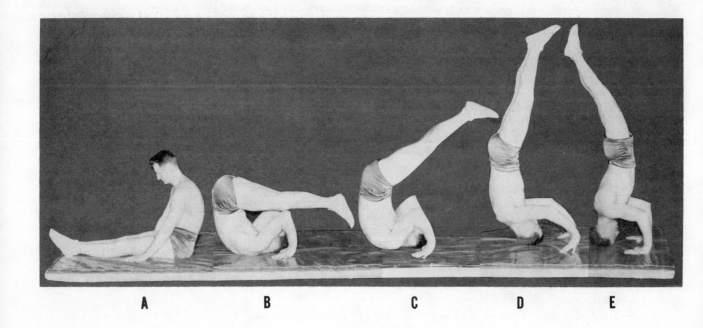

A   B   C   D   E

A—Sit down with legs bent or straight.

B—Roll backward with chin on chest.

C—When back of head touches mat, place hands by head with thumbs in.

D—Extend hips, arching back. Roll up to top of head.

E—Slide hands backward about a foot from head, placing them a shoulders' width apart.

 (Keep the toes pointed throughout the performance.)

All stunts under 31 and 32 are Backward Roll extensions. Recovery methods out of 31 are the same as those out of a Backward Roll-2.

Learning Procedure

If you do not roll far enough, duck your head and roll downward to starting position. Start again.

If you roll too far, press hard on hands to stop roll. Then bring knees to chest, keeping feet off mat. Slowly extend legs and hips into a Headstand-5.

Spotting Technique

Stand at side of mat. As performer rolls backward, grasp ankle nearest you and assist by lifting him into a Headstand.

a. Into Neckstand

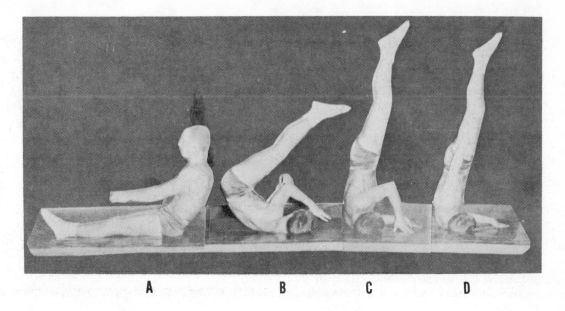

A   B   C   D

A—Stand straight. Bend forward and sit down with straight legs.

B—Roll backward. As shoulder blades touch, place right side of face on mat and reach across with left arm.

C—Extend hips and roll over onto right shoulder. Extend right arm backward, placing back of hand down. Place left hand down to control balance.

D—When balance is attained, place straight left arm on side of body.

Methods of Recovery

(1) Bend at hips and roll forward. Bend knees and place feet down. Rise to a stand.

(2) Place left hand down again as in picture C. Stretch body upward and bring right arm around to side. Roll over backward through a Fishflop-31b to a stand.

b. Fishflop (Chestroll)

Method One

Perform a Backward Roll into a momentary Headstand. (Do not hold the balance.) Lift head and shoulders forward. Roll over chest, front of body and thighs. As you touch thighs, push off with hands, bend at hips and knees and jump to a stand. You may remain in a front support position instead of rising to a stand.

Method Two

From a sitting position, roll to the back. Extend legs upward, straightening hips. Tilt head to left side and roll over right side of face with or without use of hands. Snap to a stand as described under Method One.

Learning Procedure

(1) Do a Headstand. Lift the head and shoulders forward and perform last part of Fishflop and the Chestroll Backward-30 to a stand. This is pictured on the preceding page.

(2) Perform the Backward Roll into a Headstand-31. Hold it. Then perform (1) of the learning procedure above.

Spotting Technique

Same as for Backward Roll into Headstand-31. In addition, hold performer's ankle as he rolls over front of body. This should keep him from crashing down on front of body in a piked position.

32. Backward Roll into a Handstand week 4

A—Sit down with legs straight and toes pointed downward. Place hands down with thumbs in.

   Roll backward with legs straight and chin on chest.

B —Lift hands off and place them by head with thumbs in.

C—Extend hips and push upward with hands.

D—Straighten arms and rise into a Handstand-16. Lift head upward.

Learning Technique is the same as for Backward Roll into Headstand-31.

Spotting Technique is also the same as for Backward Roll into Headstand.

60

33. Double Elbow Lever

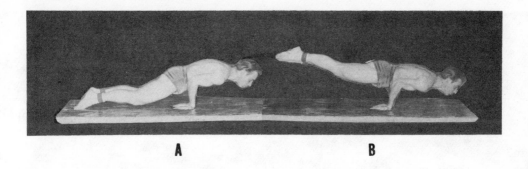

A   B

A—Kneel down. Place elbows against groin just inside hip bones and place hands together on mat with thumbs out.

B—Lift feet and head up and arch back.

Methods of Recovery

(1) Return to a kneeling position. Then rise to a stand.

(2) Slowly turn hands in and raise body into a Handstand. This is the same as the Scale into a Handstand-16j.

Girls have little use for the levers.

a. Single Elbow Lever

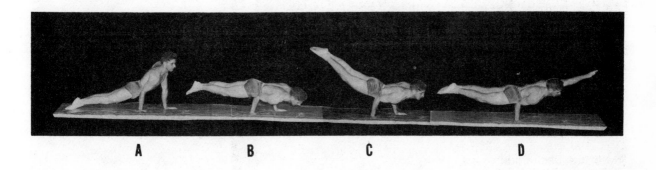

A   B   C   D

A—Kneel down. Place right elbow against groin just inside hip bone. Place right hand down with thumb forward and left hand down with thumb in. Extend legs.

B—Support body with arms.

C—Lean forward, lift legs up and arch body.

D—Slowly raise left arm forward and shift body weight completely over right arm.

Methods of Recovery

(1) Use the same recovery as (1) above.

(2) Turn body to right and place left hand down on same line with right hand. Perform a Scale into a Handstand-16j.

34. Kip (Snap-up) (Shoulderspring)

A   B   C   D   E

A—Lie down. Raise straight legs upward and roll backward into a Pretzel Bend—preliminary stunt 1. (This position is also called the Kip position.) Place hands on mat with thumbs in. Roll downward until shoulder blades touch mat, keeping hands in contact with mat.

B—Kick straight legs upward and outward.

C—At the same time, push off forcefully with hands and arch the back.

D—Land on balls of feet with toes pointed outward, with feet under body and knees straight. The shock of landing should be absorbed in hips and not back.

E—Keep arms stretched overhead with head back.

Learning Procedure

Get into a Kip (Pretzel Bend) position. Slowly roll downward and kick legs outward, keeping hands on mat. Place feet down with toes turned out. As feet touch mat, lift shoulders straightening arms. You are now in a Backbend (High Bridge)—preliminary stunt 2b. Rock forward to a stand by pushing forward with hands.

(This method is effective in teaching the performer when and how to push.)

Spotting Technique

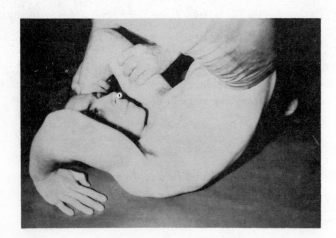

Kneel on right knee at left side of performer with left leg extended sideward. Grasp left upper arm of performer with right hand and wrist with left hand. Direct the performer when to kick. As he does, lift him off mat by arm and hold him up until his feet touch mat.

Use two spotters.

When performer becomes more skilled, spotters should give him less assistance.

Once the Kip is learned well, the following variations may be practiced with spotting.

a. With Hands on Thighs (Snap-up) (Shoulderspring)

A—Lie down in a Kip position with hands on thighs.

B—Roll downward until shoulder blades touch mat. Then kick straight legs upward and outward, pushing on thighs.

C—Arch back, but not excessively.

D—Land with knees bent and toes turned slightly outward.

b. Without Hands (Snap-up) (Shoulderspring)

This stunt is the same as 34a, with the exception that arms are held out to side during performance.

c. With Half Twist (Kip Half)

A—Lie down in Kip position and place hands on mat by head.

B—Kick straight legs upward, turning hips counterclockwise (to the left).

C—At the same time, push off with hands, bringing right arm across chest and left arm under body.

D—Land in a front support (Push-up position-strength stunt 1) with arms straight and head up.

Kneel at right side. Grasp right side with left-hand thumb up and left side with right hand also thumb up. As performer kicks, pull toward you with right hand and push with left.

35. Neckspring

A   B   C   D

A—Lower into a Straddle position-7 with hands on mat directly under shoulders. Bend arms, placing back of head on mat.

B—Roll forward to shoulder blades, dropping hips and maintaining contact with hands.

C—Perform the Kip-34.

D—Land on balls of feet with toes pointed outward and knees bent. Keep arms stretched overhead.

As greater flexibility is developed, performer should land with straight legs.

Spotting technique is the same as for Kip-34.

a. With Hands on Thighs

Get into a Straddle position-7 with hands on thighs. Lean forward slowly placing back of head on mat. Roll forward and perform Kip with hands on thighs-34a.

b. Without Hands

This stunt is the same as 35a above with the exception that arms are held out to sides and not used during performance.

c. With Half Twist (Neckspring Half)

This stunt is the same as the Kip with a Half Twist-34c with the exception that it is preceded by a roll forward from a Straddle position-7.

36. Headspring

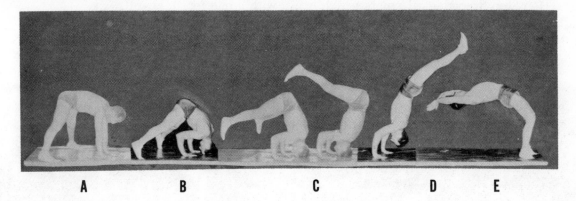

A—Do a Straddle-7, placing hands down.

B—Lean forward and bend arms.

Straighten knees and place top of head on mat.

C—Shift hips ahead of hands and kick legs up and over arching back.

D—Push off with hands.

E—Land on balls of feet with knees straight and arms raised overhead.

Learning Procedures

(1) Do Headstand Bridgeover-24a; kick to Headstand from both feet. Then speed it up, pushing off with hands. Use two spotters.

(2) Do Headspring off a rolled mat with two spotters.

The spotting technique is the same as for the Forward Handspring-38.

37. Hop Step

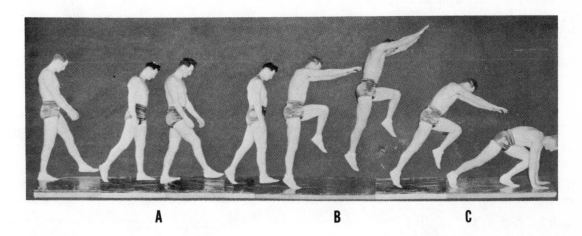

A—Walk forward on left foot and then right.

B—Raise straddle left leg and spring upward off ball of right.

C—Land on right foot and step forward on left leg, bending it. Place hands down about a foot ahead with shoulders ahead of hands.

(When Hop Step is learned effectively, it may be preceded by a run instead of a walk.)

This stunt is relatively easy. However, it is included here because it is most logically learned with the Forward Handspring-38 which follows.

The Hop Step precedes all stunts which begin with a one foot take-off.

38. Forward Handspring

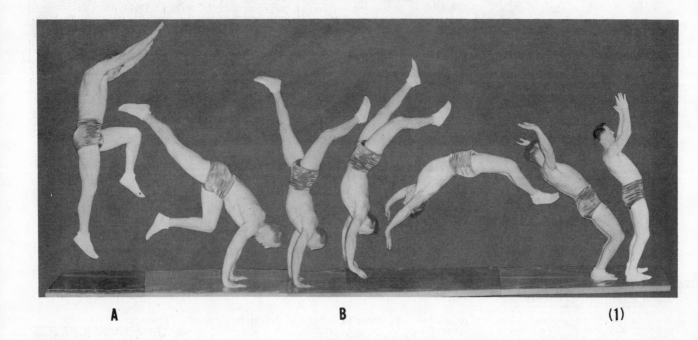

A   B   (1)

A—Perform a Hop Step-37.

B —Kick straight right leg upward and at same time, push off with hands and with left foot.

   (This part of the stunt is done rapidly and forcefully.)

   Keep head back with back arched.

Methods of Recovery

   (1) Land with arms raised overhead.

   (2) Land controlled on right foot with straight left leg raised. From it a performer can do stunts which require a one-footed take-off.

   (This landing is called a Walkout. It places performer in position to do stunts which require a take-off from one foot. See page 176, Routine 12, Picture 7.)

Learning Procedures

Do Forward Limberover-24 many times. Using spotters, do it more rapidly until a Handspring is done.

Spot as you do for regular Forward Handspring. Admonish performer not to bend his arms and to keep his head back.

Spotter should sit on left side of rolled mat ready to place left arm around performer's chest should he overturn.

A tumbler with good flexibility can learn a Forward Handspring Walkout by doing the Forward Walkover faster and faster. This is especially true of girl tumblers.

As soon as possible tumbler should push off forcefully instead of bridging over.

Spotting Technique

Kneel on right knee at right side of performer with left leg extended sideward. Place left hand on performer's left arm with thumb down and right hand on lower back with thumb up. Spotter at left side does just opposite. As performer springs off, lift him. Then hold him up until he lands on his feet.

a. With One Hand

This stunt is the same as the Forward Limberover with One Hand-24b, except that it is performed rapidly and forcefully.

b. Diving

Take off from both feet after landing out of a Hurdle-22 or a Handspring. Overturn Handspring or lean forward after landing out of Hurdle. Spring, throwing arms down toward legs. Land in a piked position. Quickly arch body and spring to a stand. This stunt requires great speed and lean on take-off.

39. Tinsica

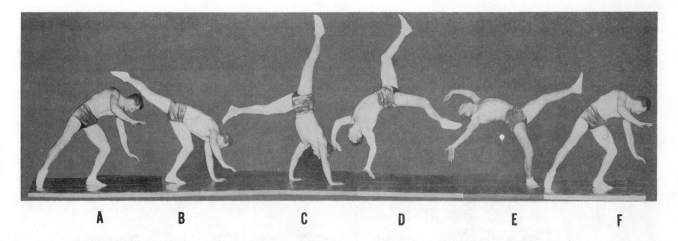

A B C D E F

A—Perform a Hop Step-37, landing with arms overhead and straight left leg raised forward.

B —Bend left knee and kick straight right leg upward. Place left hand down with thumb in about a foot in front of left foot.

C—Push off with left foot and place right hand on mat about a foot ahead of and to side of left hand.

D—Push off with left hand and then with right.

E —Turn over forward with back arched. Place right foot on mat under body with right hip extended and knee straight.

F —Rise with arms raised overhead. Lower left leg and place it in front and to side of right leg. This leg action is referred to as a Walkout.

Correct performance of the Tinsica is dependent on momentum and a forceful push.

To do the stunt correctly, the performer must turn straight over forward.

A nice effect is to develop a rhythmical 1, 2, 3, 4 beat by placing hands and feet down in an even, rapid tempo.

Learn a series of fast Tinsicas without a pause between the Walkout [see Methods of Recovery (2) under Forward Handspring-38] and the step with left foot into the next Tinsica.

Learning Procedure

   (1) Perform a Forward Handspring-38, landing on right foot first and then left. This one-two step of the feet is called a Walkout.

   (2) Perform a Forward Handspring, but this time place hands as for Tinsica, right hand ahead of left.

After learning steps (1) and (2) properly, combine them into a Tinsica.

a. With One Hand

It is the same as two-handed Tinsica except right hand is placed in the center of mat, and left is held sideward.

b. Spotters

Do the same as the Spotting Forward Walkovers-26b.

c. Diving

Same as Diving Forward Walkover-26d except place hands down one at a time and do Walkover much faster.

40. Backward Handspring (Flipflop)

A   B   C   D   E   F

A—Stand erect with feet about six inches apart and with arms raised slightly forward.

B —Smoothly swing arms backward as far as possible and sit down without leaning forward or pushing knees forward. Keep body at right angles to thighs and thighs at right angles to lower legs, like sitting in a chair.

   (This position is the preparatory sit for the Backward Handspring.)

C—Forcefully swing arms forward, upward and backward. Spring off balls of feet, throw head backward and hips forward.

D—Dive through a Handstand-16.

E—Land with weight on heels of hands about two feet back from take-off spot with shoulders stretched, arms straight and thumbs in.

F—Do Snapdown-18 to a stand and raise arms forward.

Always do the handspring smoothly and rapidly.

If you land too low out of the dive, you are not pushing off with feet.

Keep from going too high by throwing head and hips early; however, do not eliminate the push-off with feet.

If you lean forward on preparatory sit, you will gain forward on dive backward. This will make it difficult to complete the handspring.

If you do not sit low enough, you will dive too high; if you sit too low, you will jam your wrists when you land on your hands out of dive.

If you lean backward too much on sit, you will have a tendency to cast (dive) backward.

Learn Backward Handspring before Backward Somersault-45, because layout stunt, like Handspring, is harder to learn when a tuck stunt like a Somersault has been learned previously.

Learning Procedures and Spotting Techniques

A   B

(1) A—Spotter one stands at left side of performer with his right hand on lower back and left hand on back of performer's knee. Spotter two stands at right side and places his left hand on top of spotter one's right hand and his right hand on back of thigh.

B—Both spotters lift performer off mat and hold him firmly through turn over backward. In this way, when he lands on heel of his hands, he will not jam his wrists.

When performer is safely in Handstand both spotters take hands away.

Performer has actually done a Backward Limberover-27, with assistance.

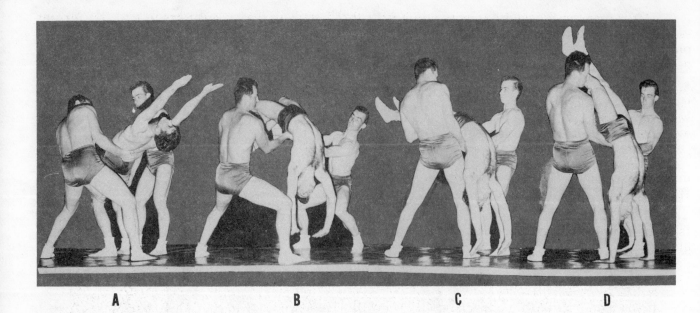

A   B   C   D

(2) A—Spotters place their hands on performer in manner described in first step. Performer bends his knees slightly and leans backward against spotters' hands with his head back and his arms raised overhead.

B—At a signal from one spotter, performer springs backward arching his back.

C—Spotters keep their hands on performer's back as he springs backward so as to maintain contact with his lower back.

D—When performer is safely through Handstand, spotters may remove their hands.

Performer ends the stunt with a Snapdown-18.

A

(3) Spotters place their hands on performer as described in step (1). Performer sits in a deep squat with his arms hanging at his sides and leans backward against spotters' hands. He swings his arms forward, upward and backward forcefully and springs off balls of feet into Backward Handspring.

After many successful attempts at the first three steps of the learning procedure, performer is ready to try the complete Backward Handspring. This time the spotters unclasp their hands and place them on performer's lower back on side nearest them. The rest of spotting technique is same as described on opposite page.

As performer does preparatory sit keep right hand on his lower back. If you let your right hand move upward as performer sits, it would rest on his shoulder blades and impede his backward turn over.

See pages 1, 2 and 4 for an explanation of belt-spotting techniques.

If you apply too much pressure on pelvic region during spotting, performer may rely too much on your help. Too much pressure on his lower back may cause him to throw forward as he springs.

As performer becomes more capable, keep right hand a few inches from his back. Admonish him not to lean back on the sit in search of the hand. As he springs, move right hand against his back.

One-Man Spotting

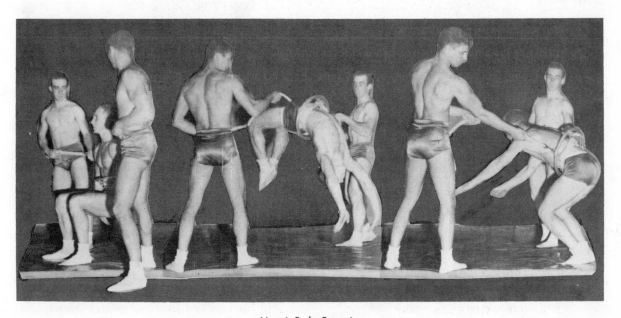

Hand-Belt Spotting

71

If the performer twists to one side while doing the Backward Handspring (without spotting or with one spotter), he should be required to relearn the stunt with two spotters. Two spotters can usually offset any tendency the performer might have to twist. It should be emphasized that the performer must push off equally with both feet and throw his arms and head straight back.

The following variations should not be attempted until the stunt is performed effectively.

a. With Half Twist

Start a Backward Handspring. As you land in a momentary Handstand, from dive backward, push off with hands and do a Snapdown with a Half Twist-20a. (See pictures in Chapter 4, Routine 9.)

b. Into Handstand

Do a preparatory sit. (See picture B, page 68, under Backward Handspring.) Swing arms forward, upward and backward, and spring slightly forward off balls of feet. Do not swing arms as hard as you do for regular Handspring. Throw head backward and hips forward, arching body. Land in an underbalanced Handstand. Lift head upward, press hard on finger tips and pull body into a balanced Handstand.

c. Into Chestroll

Perform a Backward Handspring into Handstand, holding handstand momentarily. Bend arms, push shoulders forward and gently lower chest to mat. Roll through last part of Backward Chestroll-30.

Spotting Technique

As performer does Backward Handspring, two spotters, one on either side, reach in with both hands and grasp his ankles. Spotting helps performer slow up his Backward Handspring so he can roll through Backward Chestroll in a controlled manner.

d. One-Handed

This stunt is done the same as the two-handed Backward Handspring. The only exception is that left hand is kept off mat during performance. A series of back handsprings can be done with alternate hands placed down.

e. Cradle

A

B

C

D

A—Do preparatory sit for Backward Handspring. Swing arms forward, upward and backward.

B—At same time spring upward and backward, keeping chin on chest. (Do not throw head back.)

Land on hands with arms straight in an underbalanced handstand.

C—Lower into a Kip position-34.

D—Immediately perform a Kip to a stand on two feet or as pictured.

This stunt is done smoothly and in a continuous manner.

Instead of kipping forward, performer may Kip backward into a Handstand.

Spotting Technique

Spotter at left side of performer kneels on right knee and extends left leg sideward. He grasps performer's left upper arm with left hand and places back of right hand on mat.

Spotter on other side does the opposite. Performer rolls backward into a Kip position so his shoulder blades rest on spotters' hands. Performer does a Kip-34, to a bent knee stand with assistance from spotters. Then he performs a Cradle from a deep squat position. Spotters catch him on shoulder blades and lower him to mat as he places hands down. Performer then does a Kip to a stand without assistance.

Girls generally have difficulty performing the Forward Somersault-44 and its variations because they lack the strength. They should postpone the learning of these stunts and spend their time on the next three stunts which require flexibility more than strength.

41. Aerial Cartwheel

A

B

C

A—Run sideward ending run on right foot. Perform a Hop Step-37. Bend forward, throwing arms downward with left arm leading. Kick straight right leg overhead and push off with ball of left foot.

B—Do a Cartwheel-3 without touching hands to mat.

C—Land on ball of right foot with it turned backward. Pivot on it. Turn and face forward. Step on left foot.

Performance pictured is opposite to description.

Learning Procedure

Do a diving Cartwheel with one hand, 3a, cutting it back. Repeat it many times until you can perform the Aerial Cartwheel.

Notice how wide legs are straddled in picture B. A good Straddle-7 enables you to get your right leg over and down, making the execution easier.

Spotting Technique

See page 87. Technique is the same as for Sideward Somersault-46.

a. Aerial Cartwheel (Standing)

This stunt is performed the same as the Aerial Cartwheel from a run. The only difference is that preliminary to take-off performer bends forward, touching chest to left thigh and raising straight leg overhead. (Just before take-off, he is in an inverted Split.) This position makes the turnover sideward easier from a stand. When Aerial Cartwheel is performed from a run, the extreme bend and leg raise are not as important.

42. Kickover (Aerial Walkover)

A

B

C

D

E

A—Run forward and do a Hop Step-37.

B—Bend forward, throwing arms downward.

C—Kick straight right leg overhead and push off with ball of left foot.

D—Lift shoulders upward and perform a Walkover-26 without touching hands to mat.

E—Land with right leg placed under body and with back arched. Lean forward straightening up to a stand. Place left foot down. (Explanation is opposite to what is pictured above.)

Learning Procedure

Do a diving Forward Walkover with one hand (right hand)-26b, cutting it back. Repeat this stunt over and over until you can take right hand away and perform an aerial.

Spotting Technique

Use two spotters. Spotter on right grasps right shoulder with right hand thumb up and right upper arm with left hand thumb up. Spotter on other side does opposite. Spotters should squat down. They should support performer, not lift him. Tumbler is supposed to hold bent arms down while running so spotters can grasp them when he reaches them.

At first, spot a standing Aerial Walkover to learn the spotting technique.

When tumbler performs capably, spot only shoulder, allowing him to swing straight arms through.

Notice split legs in picture D. A good Split-6 is important in getting right leg up, over and under body.

a. Kickover (Standing)

This stunt is performed the same as the Kickover from a run. The only difference is that preliminary to the take-off the performer bends forward as described for the Aerial Cart Wheel (Standing)-41a.

77

43. Barani (Aerial Roundoff)

A

B

A—The take-off is the same as for the Aerial Kickover-42.

    Lift shoulders upward. Perform diving Roundoff-19b, without touching hands to mat.

B—Land on both feet under body with knees bent.

Learning Procedure

Perform a diving Roundoff with one hand (right hand)-19c, cutting it back. Repeat it many times until you are able to do it without using hands.

Spot this stunt in a twisting belt if not successful with diving Roundoff.

Girls will have more success with the Aerial Walkover, Cart Wheel and Roundoff than with the Forward and Backward Somersaults 44 and 45.

a. Barani (Standing)

Perform Barani from a stand same as from a run. Only difference is that preliminary to take-off bend forward in manner described for the Aerial Cart Wheel (Standing)-41a.

44. Forward Somersault (Front Sommie—Front Flip)

a. From a Run

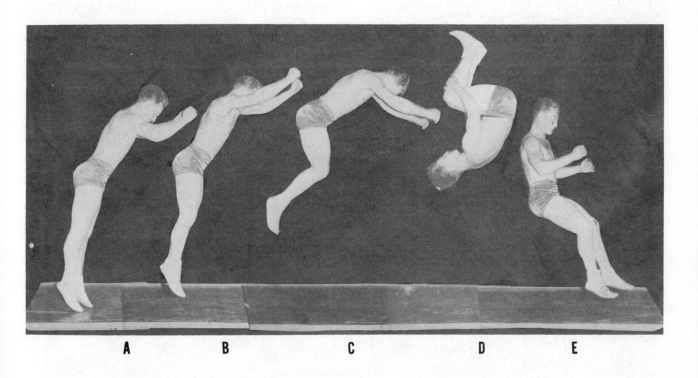

A—Take a fast run, ending on left foot. Do a Hurdle Step-22, and land with a slight lean forward.

B—Spring up off balls of feet and forcefully extend arms upward, bringing knees up to chest.

C—At peak of spring, drive arms down forcefully.

D—Duck head and grasp legs a few inches below knees. Pull legs in and back.

E—When you have completed somersault (you are in an upright position), release grasp on legs and land on balls of feet with knees bent and body relaxed. Raise arms overhead and hold head back to keep from overturning somersault.

Do not cover more than three feet from take-off to point of landing.

If you lean to one side during the performance, relearn the stunt with spotting, making an effort to turn over straight.

A picture of a practice spring for the Forward Somersault is shown at the left.

Learning Procedure

(1) Roll up 20 feet of old mat tightly and place it across a tumbling mat. Stand facing rolled mat. Place hands down near rolled mat and duck head in front of it. Push off with hands and do a Forward Roll-1 over mat. Keep tucked throughout performance and land in a sitting position on mat with knees turned out. (Keep knees out to avoid hitting chin on landing.)

(2) Stand far enough from rolled mat, so that after you do a Hurdle Step you land just a few inches from it. Hold arms overhead while doing Hurdle Step. Spring up (do not dive out) and try to do somersault without touching rolled mat. At first land sitting on rolled mat. After you do somersault over rolled mat many times without landing on it, remove mat and do it without mat, with spotting.

Spotting Technique

Two spotters sit on either end of rolled mat, facing each other. Spotter at left side places his right hand with thumb in against performer's hip and left on performer's shoulder blade. Spotter on right places his hands in an opposite manner.

Performer bends forward with arms down. He throws arms back, ducks head and springs off balls of feet. Spotters support him with hands on his hips and turn him over with hands on his shoulder blades. As he lands, spotter on left slides his right arm across his chest to keep him from overturning somersault. Spotter on right uses his left arm.

Spotters can remove rolled mat and stand up to spot in the same manner described above. Picture on opposite page shows Forward Somersault spotted by one person.

In addition to hand spotting, Hand-Belt Spotting can be used. This is described on page 2.

Spotting Technique-2. Hand-Belt Spotting (see figures on pages 1 and 2).

Spotting Technique-3. Overhead Suspension-Belt Spotting—Trolley (see Figure 3 on page 4).

Spotting Technique-4. Overhead Suspension-Belt Spotting—Stationary (see Figure 2 on page 3).

b. From a Stand

Do this stunt the same as the somersault from a run; however, on the take-off lean farther forward than you did for the running Forward Somersault to compensate for the absence of a run.

When learning it, do it on several mats piled on top of one another to ease the shock of landing.

The spotting technique for a Standing Forward Somersault is pictured on the preceding page. This is the same spotting technique described before for the Forward Somersault.

Attempt this stunt after having first done stunts 45 and 46.

A   B   C   D   E

The above pictures show a running Forward Somersault with a Walkout. The performer lands (picture D) on his right leg with his left leg held high. In picture E, he leans forward and steps on left foot, shifting weight from right leg to left. This foot action is called a Walkout; it is described under the Tinsica-39.

c. With Half Twist (Running)

The performer in the pictures below does the twist to the right (clockwise); however, the twist will be described to the left. This discrepancy should not cause the performer any difficulty if he turns in the direction he has turned before whether it be right or left.

A   B

A—Start Forward Somersault.

B—Halfway through somersault, turn head left and bring right arm across chest, pull left elbow back and turn hips quickly. Do this action practically simultaneously, starting with head and working down.

Land in an erect position with the knees slightly bent.

(Throw the somersault as hard as possible.)

Do not twist too early or too late. Wait until you reach an upside-down position.

Do not lean to left on somersault or push right hip out to right side. If you do your body will move to the right, making it difficult for you to twist properly and causing you to land off mat.

On any twisting somersault make certain the somersault passes through a vertical plane.

45. Backward Somersault (Back Sommie)

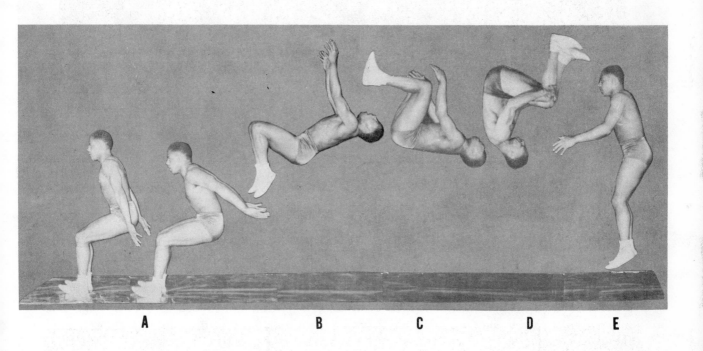

A   B   C   D   E

A—Stand erect with arms raised slightly forward, feet about six inches apart. Swing arms backward and do a Preparatory Sit without leaning or pushing knees forward. (Just like sit for Backward Handspring-40, but do not sit as deeply.)

B—Swing arms forward and upward, springing off balls of feet.

C—Bring knees up to outstretched hands.

D—Throw head backward; grasp legs just below knees, pulling legs forcefully backward and downward.

E—Complete somersault. Release grasp on legs and land on balls of feet with knees bent in a relaxed manner and with arms raised forward.

Do not throw head too soon on take-off. This will cut the height of somersault.

If you wait too long after the take-off to throw the head, you will have difficulty completing the somersault.

If you twist or lean to one side during the performance, relearn the stunt with spotting, concentrating on going straight over.

83

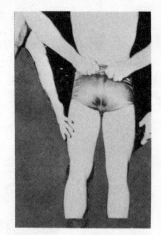

A   B

Spotter at left side of performer has right leg forward and left back. Spotter at left side of performer grasps top of his trunks with right hand. During the performance, spotter places his right hand on back of performer's knee. Spotter at other side does the opposite. Pictured also is a rear view of picture A above.

At first performer does a preparatory sit and springs upward with his arms lifted upward. He does this several times to get the idea of springing upward before turning somersault. See picture A above.

As performer does somersault, spotters support him with hands placed on trunks until he lands properly. With the other hand spotters can help performer over by throwing his legs. See picture B above.

Pictures below show one man spotting. Even though technique is the same as above, they are displayed because spotter's hands might be observed more easily in these.

Spotters assist performer with hand belt in the same way as for the Forward Somersault-44. See pages 1, 2, 3 and 4.

a. With Half Twist (Standing)

Perform a fast somersault. When you reach an inverted position, turn head left, throw right arm across chest and left elbow back. Also twist hips left, completing half twist (180 degrees).

Twist is performed easier if knees are not grasped during performance. This leaves arms free for twisting; however, knees must be kept up.

There are faults which occur in Forward Somersault twisting which are pointed out under Forward Somersault with Half Twist-44c. They occur in backward twisting as well and should be noted again and avoided.

Spotting Technique

It is almost the same as for the straight somersault. One spotter is needed who stands on right side of performer (he is going to twist to left), and places his left hand on far side of performer's lower back. The only difference is that halfway through somersault the spotter pulls his hand toward himself, helping performer twist instead of throwing him straight over. With his right hand he throws performer's legs over.

b. Backward Somersault Gaining Forward (Gainer)

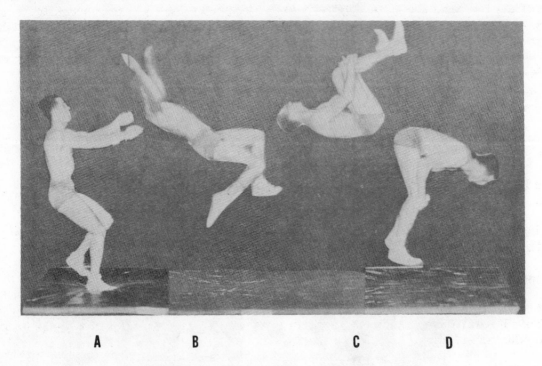

A   B   C   D

Stand with arms hanging down at sides. Walk forward on right foot.

A—Kick straight left leg forward forcefully and swing arms forward, upward and backward.

B —Throw head back. At same time, spring off with right foot and bring both legs to hands.

C—Grasp legs just below knees and pull them over to complete somersault.

D—Land with knees slightly bent.

The stunt can be done with a bent knee kick as pictured above, but it can be done more effectively with a straight leg kick on the take-off.

Spotting Technique

Spot this stunt the same as the regular Backward Somersault. Since the performer will be gaining forward on the somersault, he will have difficulty completing it at first. Follow him with hands as he goes forward. Then whip him over.

c. With Full Twist (Standing)

Do a fast somersault with fairly straight body. On take-off turn head, arms and hips a quarter turn to left but keep both feet pointed forward. Continue twist by forcing head, arms and hips farther around counterclockwise (left). Complete full twist when somersault is three quarters finished. Now bend hips and knees deeply and prepare to land as easily as possible on balls of feet.

Twist should be done smoothly—not in two halves.

Don't lean back too much on take-off or throw head back too soon.

The Backward Somersault with Full Twist from a standing take-off is one of the most difficult of tumbling stunts. Performer must have a high, fast, standing somersault (Whipback— see page 173) to be able to perform stunt successfully. (A Whipback is a fast backward somersault performed in an open-piked position. It is similar to a fast backward handspring done high enough so the hands cannot touch.)

Best method of spotting this stunt is with a twisting belt. Spotter at left side grasps rope with his left hand about two feet from belt. He places his right hand about six inches from belt. Spotter at right side does just the opposite. When tumbler reaches an upside-down position, spotter on left side steps in toward performer with right foot and slides his right hand in toward him. Other spotter does just the opposite. This puts them in position to support performer.

46. Sideward Somersault (Side Sommie)

Run forward ending run on right foot. Take a short hop forward, turning body and right foot right sideward.

Place left foot down parallel to right and spring off balls of both feet alternately. At same time, stretch arms left sideward and throw head sideward.

Lift legs to hands and grasp them just below knees. Throw head left and perform somersault. Land on balls of feet with knees slightly bent.

You must go straight over sideward on the somersault.

Land on both feet or on one at a time, right preceding left, to do a Walkout (similar to Walkout from Forward Somersault-44, described on page 82 with the exception one is forward while other is sideward).

Spotting Technique

Stand at right side of mat and as performer reaches you, place left hand with thumb down against his right side at waist. Reach across with right arm and grasp his waist on left side with thumb down. Turn performer over by pulling on his left side and pushing up on his right.

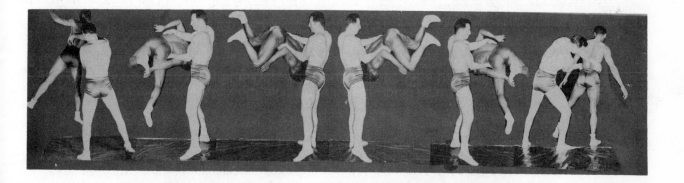

The Sideward Somersault can be performed from a stand as well as from a run just as the Forward Somersault-44.

47. Front Planche with Straight Arms

A   B   C

A—Kick into a Handstand-16.

B—Slowly lower straight body with straight arms, pushing shoulders forward.

C—As you reach a point just above horizontal, stop and tighten muscles, hold. Lower to mat and return to a stand.

Learning Procedure

(1) Kick up from Push-up position (preliminary strength stunt-1) into a Planche with legs straddled. As you kick up lean forward. Hold. Repeat many times.

(2) Do Planche with one leg straight and other bent. Reverse legs. Keep doing this over and over.

a. Front Planche with Bent Arms

This stunt is done the same as the Front Planche with straight arms. The only difference is that you bend your arms and turn your hands so thumbs point out. The arms must be free of body. Naturally, the bent arm Planche is easier than the straight arm Planche.

48. Backward Planche

Kick or press into a Handstand-16. Slowly overbalance Handstand. Counterbalance overbalance by pulling shoulders back. Continue lowering body until horizontal position is reached. Now bring head up between arms. Tighten muscles and hold. Slowly return to Handstand or lower feet to mat into Limberover-24.

49. Sideward Planche with One Arm

Start facing forward with left foot forward. Bend forward over straight left leg. Place left hand down about a foot ahead with thumb pointing forward.

Continue leaning, raising straight right leg to a horizontal position. Slowly raise left leg to right. Arch back a great deal and lock left shoulder. Hold.

Lower left leg to floor and rise to stand, or raise body into a Handstand. Then lower feet to floor.

Another way to go into Sideward Planche is from a Handstand. Lower slowly sideward into a horizontal position.

The three planches are easier to perform on the floor than on mat because the floor provides a better gripping surface.

The performer needs tremendous strength to do the Forward and Sideward Planches and great back flexibility to do the Back Planche. A flexible back helps in the performance of the Sideward Planche also.

Chapter 3

Doubles Tumbling and Balancing

Doubles tumbling and balancing stunts will be presented as were the singles stunts in progressing order from the easiest to the most difficult.   Follow this order as much as possible. After practicing the first twenty singles stunts many times, start on the first ten doubles stunts. From this point on you can mix the singles with the doubles governing yourself by your future plans.

Girls should avoid bottom men roles because these usually require quite a bit of strength. They should not do levers and similar stunts for this reason.   They should do balance and flexibility doubles stunts—stunts in which they can excel.

Doubles stunts generally are named for the action of the tumbler or balancer.   There are two types of stunts, unlike and like.   Unlike refers to the difference in size between the thrower or bottom man and the tumber or top man.   The former is the bigger of the two.   The letter U represents the word unlike and appears as the first of two letters in parentheses before the number and name of the stunt if the letter L does not appear in its place.

Like refers to the similarity in size between two tumblers or balancers.   The letter L represents the word like.

A second letter will appear in the parentheses; it will be either T for tumbling or B for balancing.

If both the U and the L appear, it means the stunt can be performed by people of unlike (U) or like (L) size.

(U-B)   1.   Front Angel Balance on Feet (Front Scale)

A   **B**   **C**

A—Bottom man lies down on mat with arms and legs raised upward.

Top man leans forward.   Bottom man grasps his hands and places his feet slightly turned out on his groin.

B —He pulls on top man's hands and raises him off mat into a horizontal balance. He releases top man's hands while latter raises arms sideward. Top man arches back, keeping legs together.

If top man is overbalanced, bottom man should push upward with balls of his feet.

Bottom man grasps top man's hands and gently lowers him back to mat or through an Assisted Limberover-24 (singles). Top man's hands touch mat.

Spotting Technique

Spotters should grasp upper arm and small of back of top man in Front Angel Balance. Then guide him through a Forward Limberover. See page 49.

(U-B) 2. Back Angel Balance on Feet (Back Scale)

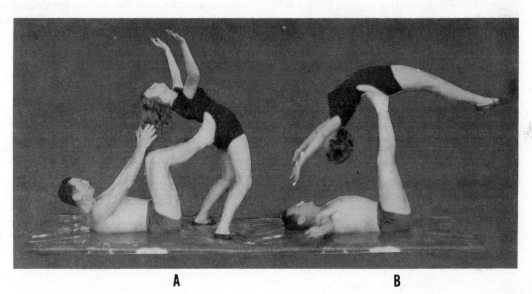

A   B

A—Bottom man lies down on his back with arms and legs raised. Top man leans against other's feet with arms raised overhead. He places his feet slightly turned out on top man's lower back.

B —Top man rocks backward and is raised off mat into a horizontal balance. He holds arch with legs together and arms sideward.

He is lowered forward to mat or does a Backward Limberover over feet and hands-27 (doubles).

Spotting Technique

Spotters should hold top man's thigh. As he is lowered through a Backward Limberover they should ease him into a momentary handstand. See pages 53 and 54.

(U-B) 3. Back Angel Straddling Waist

Both men stand, facing each other. Bottom man grasps top man's waist and lifts him. Top man straddles and wraps his legs around bottom man's waist.

He leans back into an arch. Bottom man also leans back and slowly releases his grasp. Both performers hold position.

Bottom man grasps top man by waist as top man unwraps his legs from his waist. Bottom man places him down on mat.

(U-B) 4. Front Angel Straddling Waist

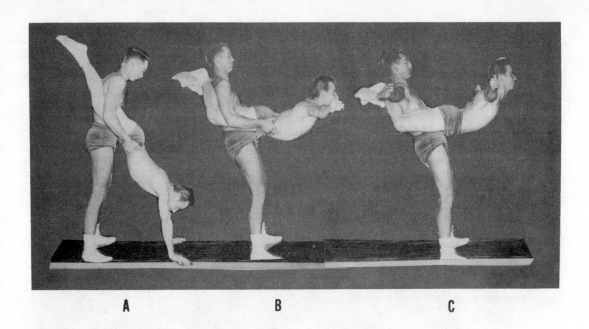

A   B   C

Start One (pictured above)

A—Top man does a Handstand-16 (singles) and opens his legs. Bottom man places his body between his legs and grasps his waist.

B —Bottom man leans back and lifts top man off mat. Top man wraps his legs around his waist.

C—When balance is attained, bottom man takes his hands away and raises his arms sideward.

Bottom man grasps top man by waist, lifts him up and places him down.

Start Two

Both men stand, facing same direction. Bottom man grasps top man by waist and lifts him off mat. Top man straddles bottom man.

(L-T) 5. Elephant Walk

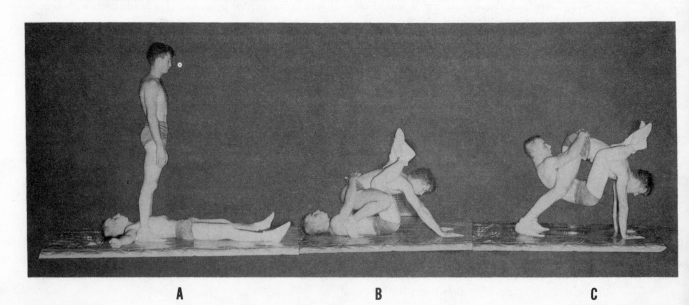

A   B   C

A—Bottom man lies down on his back. Top man straddles him.

B—Then he bends forward, placing his hands on mat between bottom man's legs. Bottom man wraps his legs around top man's waist and places his hands on his hips.

C—Top man straightens his arms and legs and walks forward, rocking from side to side simulating movements of an elephant.

At end of walk, top man kneels down again and rolls over to his back. Now top and bottom men have changed positions and are ready to walk back to their starting point.

(U-T) 6. Forward Somersault Arms Between Legs

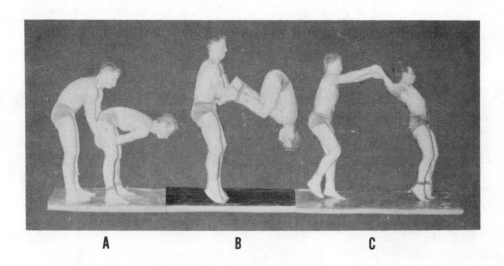

A   B   C

A—Tumbler bends forward, placing arms between legs. Thrower bends over tumbler and grasps his wrists.

B—Thrower lifts tumbler who ducks forward performing somersault in a tuck position.

C—Thrower holds tumbler high above mat, lowering him when he has completed stunt.

Spotting Technique

Grasp tumbler with both hands on upper arm. Hold him up as he is turned over. Use two spotters.

(U-T) 7. Backward Somersault by Ankle Pick-Up

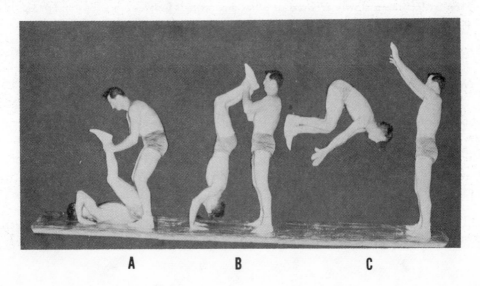

A   B   C

A—Tumbler lies down on back with legs raised upward. Thrower grasps his ankles.

B—He lifts and throws tumbler over backward.

C—Tumbler turns over with knees close to chest.

Learning Procedure

Do a slow Backward Roll into a Handstand-32 (singles) with assistance from thrower. Then perform a Snapdown-18 (singles). Continue this until you can perform stunt rapidly.

(L-T) 8. Camel Walk

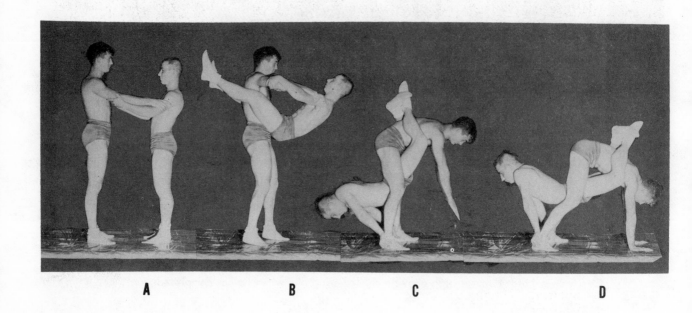

A   B   C   D

A—Both men stand face to face, grasping each other's upper arms.

B—Man on right jumps, straddles and wraps his legs around waist of man on left.

C—Man on left leans slowly forward as other man crawls between his legs and grasps his ankles.

D—Then man on left places his hands down and walks forward.

    Man on left must lean forward after other man crawls between his legs.

Another way to get into Camel Walk is to have man on right lie prone between other man's legs. Have left side performer drop to his hands and knees. Have bottom man wrap his legs around top man's waist and grasp his ankles.

Spotting Technique

Help bottom man crawl between top man's legs and watch to see that top man is leaning forward ready to fall to his hands. Don't let him fall backward.

(L-T)   9.   Forward Chain Rolls

   a. Grasping Ankles

A   B   C   D   E

A—No. 2 lies down with legs extended upward. No. 1 stands straddling his head and grasping his
   ankles with his thumbs in. No. 2 grasps No. 1's ankles in same way.

B—No. 1 leans forward, placing No. 2's feet down as No. 2 lifts him off mat.

C—As No. 1 approaches mat, he ducks his head.

D—No. 2 slowly lowers No. 1 while he rises to a stand.

E—They have completed one roll and are ready for another.

Learning Procedure

At first stunt should be learned slowly and with control. As it is perfected, the
speed of the roll should be increased.

Spotting Technique

Spotter on right places his right hand on No. 1's shoulder as he starts roll. He
helps control his roll forward. Other spotter uses his opposite hand.

   b. Grasping Feet

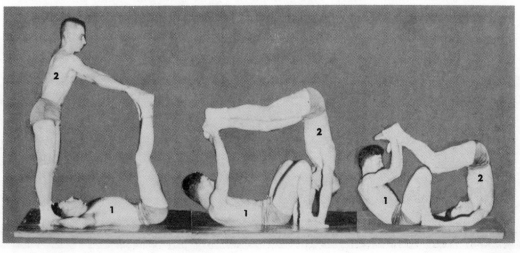

A   B   C

95

A—No. 1 lies down with legs extended upward and hands on mat with thumbs in. No. 2 stands on his hands, straddling his head and grasping his arches with thumbs in. No. 1 grasps No. 2's arches in same way.

B—No. 1 lifts No. 2 off mat and supports him. At same time, No. 2 leans forward, placing No. 1's feet down. Both maintain their grasp.

C—As No. 2 approaches mat, he ducks his head and lands on shoulders. No. 2 pulls his legs down, helping No. 1 rise to a stand. They are ready for more rolls.

Spotting Technique

Spot Forward Chain Roll grasping feet same as Forward Chain Roll grasping ankles.

$\left(\begin{smallmatrix} U \\ L \end{smallmatrix}-B\right)$ 10. Cheststand

a. On Bottom Man's Back

Method One

Bottom man kneels and places his hands down with his back straight.

Top man kneels down by bottom man's side. He rests his chest on bottom man's back and grasps his near side. He kicks or presses into a balance.

Method Two

Bottom man stands in a straddle position. He bends forward with his head up and his knees straight. He places hands on legs just above knees, keeping his arms straight.

Top man stands at side of bottom man. He leans forward and rests his chest on his back. He grasps his near side and kicks or presses into a Cheststand.

After holding balance, he returns to a stand.

[See Handstand on Back-33b (doubles).]

Spotting Technique

Spotting technique is the same as for the Headstand-5 (singles).

b. On Bottom Man's Belly

Bottom man does a Highbridge-2b (preliminary singles). Top man rests his chest on bottom man's belly. He grasps his near side and kicks into a Cheststand. (See Handstand on Belly- 33a.)

(L-T) 11. Backward Chain Rolls

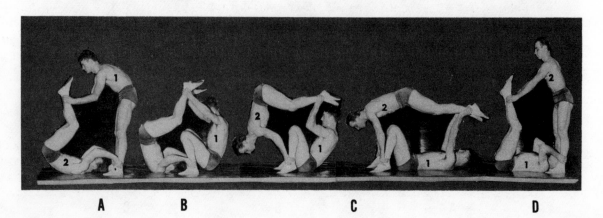

A   B   C   D

A—Both men take same position as for Forward Chain Rolls grasping ankles-9a (doubles). However, this time they face in opposite direction.

B—No. 1 (man on right) sits down quickly, placing his hips close to his feet.

C—He pulls No. 2 (man on left) upward and backward as he rolls backward, bending his arms and lifting his legs.

D—No. 2 lands on mat with feet straddling No. 1's head. Now No. 2 sits down and they continue rolling backward.

Spotting Technique

Spotter at left grasps No. 2's ankles with both hands and lifts him as for the Backward Roll to Headstand-31 (singles). Use two spotters.

(L-T) 12. Backward Limberover over Feet and Hands

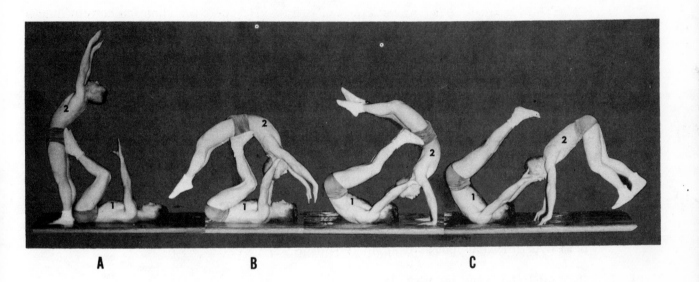

A—No. 1 lies down with his bent legs raised. No. 2 stands with his hips resting on No. 1's feet and his arms raised overhead.

B—No. 2 leans backward slowly. No. 1 grasps his shoulders and lifts him off mat.

C—No. 2 does a Backward Limberover-27 (singles) assisted by No. 1.

No. 1 does a backward roll and No. 2 sits down. Now they are ready for No. 1 to do stunt.

Stunt must be done slowly.

Spotting Technique

Spotters stand on either side of performers. Spotter on left side grasps top man's upper arm with his right hand thumb down and places his left hand with palm up against his thigh. Spotter on right side does just the opposite. These men guide the top man through the assisted Backward Limberover, so he does not roll over to the side.

$\left(\begin{smallmatrix} U \\ L \end{smallmatrix}\text{-B}\right)$ 13. Knee Shoulderstand

A   B   C

A—No. 1 lies down with knees apart and bent and with arms raised upward. No. 2 stands with right leg back, left leg between No. 1's legs and hands on No. 1's knees. No. 2 leans forward, placing shoulders on No. 1's hands.

B—He kicks with right leg and pushes off with left.

C—He rises into a balance with back arched and his head up. No. 1's arms are held straight as are No. 2's.

Top man can return to his starting position, or he can bridge over slowly to a stand.

Spotting Technique

Spotting technique is the same as for the Headstand-5 (singles). When top man limbers over forward spot as described on page 91.

(U-B) 14. Foot-to-Hand Stand (Reversed)

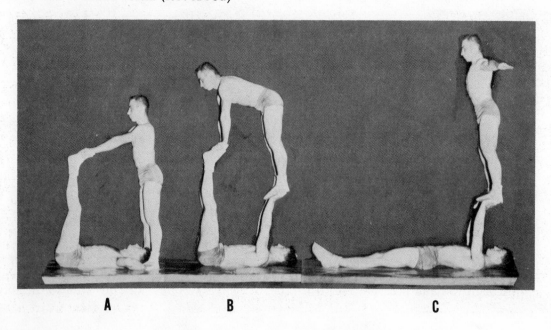

A   B   C

A—Bottom man lies down on back with bent arms raised overhead, with back of hands on mat and with legs raised upward. Top man stands on bottom man's hands, with his hands grasping bottom man's feet.

B —Bottom man presses top man upward with his arms a shoulders' width apart.

C—Top man straightens upward, raising his arms sideward. Bottom man lowers his straight legs.

Another way to perform this stunt is to have bottom man press top man into balance without top man supporting himself on bottom man's feet. Bottom man can keep his legs up during performance, lowering them when top man is up. This is the preferred way to perform the stunt.

Spotting Technique

Spotter stands at side of top man with one of his arms raised upward. If top man loses his balance, he can take hold of spotter's hand to help him regain his equilibrium.

a. Seat-on-Feet, 1/2 Turn to Foot-to-Hand

99

Top man sits on bottom man's insteps.   Then bottom man bounces him to a Seat-on-Feet.

Bottom man crosses arms so his right hand goes to other's right foot and left hand to left.   Top man turns right to a Foot-to-Hand (Reversed).

Bottom man brings legs through and top man sits on them, hooking feet on bottom man's legs.

Recovery Method

Bottom man raises straight legs upward.   Top man reaches down and grasps bottom man's feet.   He either rises to a Foot-to-Foot Stand (Reversed) or to an L support and then to a stand.

From an L support, top man can press to a Handstand-on-Feet-48 opposite to that shown on page 130.

b. Lift to Foot-to-Hand (Reversed)

Bottom man lies down placing bent arms overhead with palms up.   Top man steps on his hands with feet turned out.   Bottom man slowly presses top man to the stand.

Bottom man can raise legs to the vertical.   Then if top man loses balance, he can grasp them.

100

c. From Foot-to-Hand (Reversed) to Foot-to-Foot (Reversed)

Performers do a Foot-to-Hand.

Top man places hands on bottom man's feet, leaving room for his feet.

Putting his weight on his hands, top man carefully places his left foot behind his left hand. Then he does the same with right. Slowly he straightens up to a stand.

To get down he reverses the procedure.

d. Get-Up from Low to High Foot-to-Hand Stand

This is similar to the Get-Up from Low to High Hand-to-Hand Handstand-65, but it is much easier. Start working with a light person and progress to a heavier one.

Use two spotters.

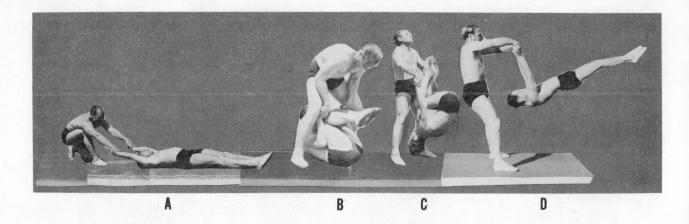

A B C D

A—With right leg forward, thrower squats behind tumbler and grasps his hands. Both men have thumbs turned in.

B—Quickly thrower steps forward with left foot and brings his right foot even with his left. He is crouched over tumbler with bent arms. At same time, tumbler bends his arms and brings his knees up to his chest.

C—Thrower snaps his straight arms upward to a horizontal position, lifting tumbler off mat in a tuck.

D—Tumbler extends his body obliquely outward with back arched.

As his legs drop, thrower releases tumbler's hands. He lands erect with knees straight and back arched.

The entire action of stunt takes place rapidly.

Spotting Technique

Spot tumbler in the same way as for the Kip-34 (singles).

a. Snapout with Half Turn

A B C D E

A—Tumbler lies down with arms crossed in front, right arm over left. He turns palms of both hands up. Thumb of left hand points to left. He twists right hand a full turn to left so his palm is up.

Thrower leans over tumbler and grasps his hands, left hand to left and right hand to right.

B—Thrower walks quickly forward until his arms are straight as tumbler bends his knees up.

C—Then thrower leans back and forcefully pulls tumbler forward between his legs. Tumbler does a half turn to right. (Both men keep their arms straight.)

D—Thrower leans slightly forward as tumbler swings back between his legs. Thrower straightens up again and snaps tumbler forward.

E—Tumbler extends his legs and straightens his hips. As he lands, thrower releases grip.

This stunt is done smoothly and continuously.

(U-B)   16.   Thighstand (Radiator Cap)

a. From L Support

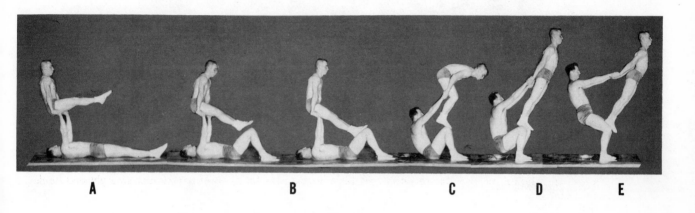

A   B   C   D   E

A—Bottom man lies down with his arms up, his elbows straight and his wrists bent back. Top man stands straddling his head. He grasps bottom man's hands with thumbs in. Bottom man may place his second finger against top man's wrist or he can squeeze top man's wrist between his index and second fingers.

Top man puts his weight on bottom man's arms, leans forward and brings his straight legs through to an L support.

B—Top man lowers his legs and places his feet on bottom man's thighs.

C—He bends forward, pulling bottom man to a sit then to a squat position.

D—He straightens his body and leans forward as bottom man leans back.

E—Bottom man rises up from a deep squat, maintaining his backward lean.

Both men keep their arms straight during performance of stunt.

Spotting Technique

Spotter stands on right side of performers. He grasps top man's upper arm and assists him into the Thighstand.

b. Lift by Waist into Free Thighstand

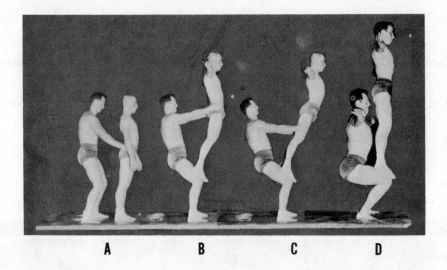

A   B   C   D

A—Bottom man stands behind top man and grasps him by waist.

B—He bends his knees, leans back and lifts top man to a stand on his thighs.

C—He slowly shifts his hands to thighs. Top man leans forward, arching his back. He raises arms sideward.

D—Bottom man straightens up and pulls top man in close, keeping his thighs at right angles to his lower legs.

Top man lowers his arms with thumbs in and palms up. Bottom man grasps top man's hands with back of his hands up. (See picture E, Thighstand, on the preceding page.)

Methods of Recovery

(1) Bottom man can lower top man to stand in front.

(2) He can lift top man to a seat on shoulders or to a stand, last picture of Shoulder Mount from Front-39.

(3) He can lift top man to a high L support from which top man can press to a High Hand-to-Hand Handstand-68, picture E.

c. Reverse Thighstand

A   B   C

A—Performers start in a Thighstand-16a. Bottom man releases grasp of top man's right hand and raises his right arm. Top man turns right, placing right foot on bottom man's left thigh. He raises his right arm sideward and both hold pose.

B—Top man turns farther to right as bottom man grasps his right hand. Top man lifts his left foot and places it on bottom man's right thigh.

C—Bottom man releases top man's left hand. They both lean back and raise their arms upward, holding Reverse Thighstand for about four counts.

Bottom man releases his grasp and top man jumps off his thighs. They turn and face sidward in same direction.

$\begin{pmatrix} U \\ L \end{pmatrix}$-B) 17. Foot-to-Foot Stand (Regular)

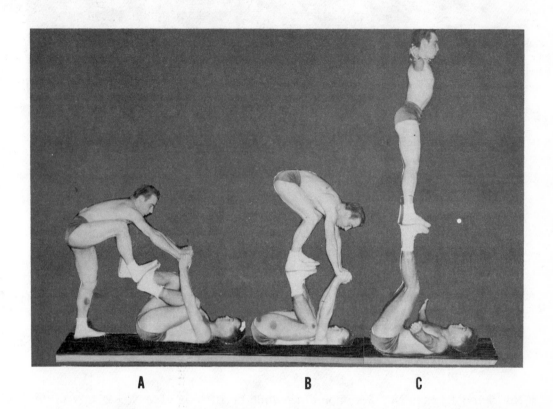

A B C

A—Bottom man lies down. Top man places his right foot against bottom man's left foot. Bottom man reaches up and grasps top man's hands.

B—Top man rocks forward slowly and places left foot against bottom man's right. He supports himself on bottom man's hands until he gains his balance.

C—Top man rises to a stand. Then bottom man slowly straightens his knees. Top man holds balance for three or four seconds.

Methods of Recovery

    (1) He jumps off bottom man's feet either forward or backward.

    (2) Top man can bend forward as bottom man bends his knees and grasp his arms to do a Low Arm-to-Arm Shoulderstand-28.

    (3) Top man can bend forward and grasp hands with bottom man and press a regular Low Hand-to-Hand Handstand-56.

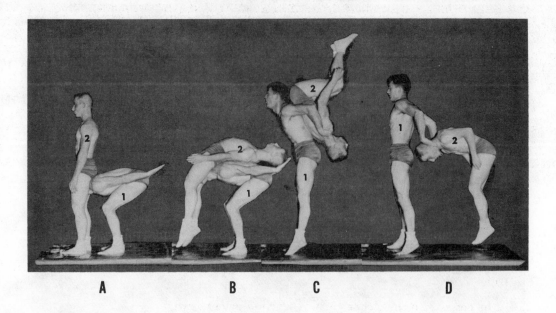

A—No. 1 bends forward and raises his arms back with palms up. He places his head between No. 2's legs. His knees are bent deeply.

B—No. 2 falls back slowly. As his shoulders touch No. 1's back, No. 1 raises his body, straightening his knees.

C—He grasps No. 2's shoulders. No. 2 bends his knees to his chest.

D—When No. 2 is in an inverted position, No. 1 lifts him upward. This action snaps him over to a stand.

No. 2 bends forward and places his head between No. 1's legs. He is ready to lift No. 1. They continue this stunt alternating top and bottom positions.

No. 1 must grasp No. 2's shoulders when he lifts or else No. 2 may slide down his back without turning the somersault.

No. 2 should hold his arms overhead in the event that No. 1 forgets to grasp his shoulders.

An easy variation of this stunt is to have No. 2, after he has lowered back slowly, reach for and place his hands on the mat. Then have No. 1 straighten up and push No. 2 slowly through the handstand. This stunt is called the Backward Limberover by neck lift.

Spotting Technique

Spotter grasps No. 2's left upper arm with both hands and No. 2's wrist with his left hand.

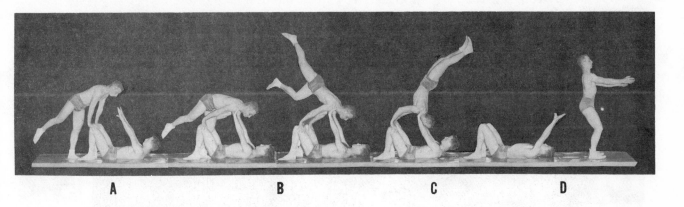

A   B   C   D

A—Thrower lies down as for Knee Shoulderstand-13. Tumbler runs forward ending run on right foot.

He performs a Hop Step-37 (singles) and places his hands on thrower's knees.

B —Thrower grasps tumbler's shoulders. Tumbler kicks his right leg up and pushes off with his left foot.

C—As he passes through balance position, thrower pushes upward.

D—Tumbler turns over and lands with his knees bent. Thrower keeps his arm overhead to protect himself should tumbler land too close to his head or fall back.

Learning Procedure

(1) Perform a Knee Shoulderstand-13. Slowly bridge over to a stand.

(2) Perform the above more rapidly without stopping in a balance position.

(3) Finally, perform the Knee Shoulderspring.

Spotting Technique

The spotting technique is the same as for the Forward Handspring-38 (singles). The only exception is that the spotters stand instead of kneeling.

a. Diving Knee Shoulderspring

This stunt is the same as the Knee Shoulderspring. The only exception is that the tumbler ends the run with a Hurdle-22 (singles) and dives into the stunt.

To add to the show value of the stunt, have a few men lie down across the mat next to the bottom man's feet. This creates a greater obstacle for the tumbler to clear.

107

Learning Procedure

Dive a few feet. Then gradually extend the distance of the dive. Postpone the learning of this stunt for a while.

(U-B) 20. Front Angel Balance (High) (Front Swan)

A—Bottom man stands with left foot ahead of right and grasps top man by waist with his palms resting on top man's pelvis.

B—As top man jumps, bottom man lifts and gets under him.

C—He straightens his arms and stretches his body.

If top man is overbalanced, bottom man can push upward with his thumbs.

Spotting Technique

Spotter should stand behind bottom man with his arms raised upward. If top man should overbalance, spotter can reach up and keep him from falling over bottom man's head. Another man should stand in front to help with the lowering.

(U-B) 21. Back Angel Balance High One-Handed

Top man stands with arms forward and left leg bent up. Bottom man stands behind with left leg ahead of right. He places right hand on pelvis and grasps left ankle with left hand. At signal top man jumps and bottom man lifts. During jump top man straightens left leg and bends right, placing right foot on left knee. Bottom man raises arm to side.

Spotting Technique

Use same spotting technique as for Front Angel Balance High-20. Be ready to catch top man in case he overbalances.

Method of Recovery

Bottom man lowers top man forward and grasps his left ankle to control the descent.

(U-B) 22. Handstand on Thighs

A—Top man stands on left side of bottom man and places his hands on his legs just above his knees. Bottom man reaches across and grasps top man's waist with his right hand thumb down. He grasps his other side with his left hand with thumb down.

B—Top man kicks up and does a quarter turn right as bottom man leans back, keeping his knees bent. He pulls top man sideward and upward into Handstand which he holds for at least four counts. Bottom man lowers him left sideward to mat.

From Front Angel Straddling Waist-4 top man can grasp bottom man's thighs and do a straddled press into a Handstand.

A   B

(L-T) 23. Back-to-Back, Rollover with Half Turn

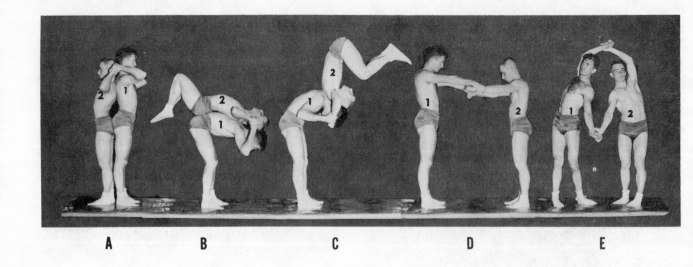

A   B   C   D   E

A—Both men stand back to back with arms raised overhead. No. 1 (man on right) reaches back and grasps No. 2's wrists with thumbs down.

B—No. 1 bends forward with his knees slightly bent. He lifts and pulls No. 2 onto his back.

C—Top man brings his knees up to his chest as he is lifted upward. No. 1 straightens up as No. 2 continues his roll backward.

D—He completes roll, landing on balls of feet with knees bent. No. 1 retains grasp on his wrists.

E—No. 1 raises his right arm upward and turns to right. No. 2 raises his left arm and turns to left. No. 1 releases grasp and No. 2 grasps his wrists.

Performers have changed positions and are ready for another rollover.

Spotting Technique

Spotters grasp No. 2's arms and guide and lift him as he rolls backward over No. 1's back.

(L-T) 24. Backward Somersault over Feet and Hands

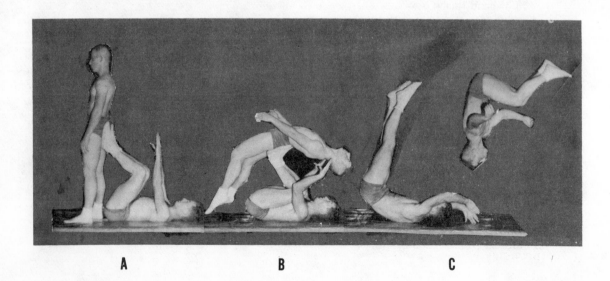

A   B   C

A—Thrower lies down with legs bent and feet against tumbler's buttocks. His arms are up ready to catch tumbler's shoulders if he does not turn somersault properly. Tumbler stands close to thrower's hips.

B—He leans and throws back, bringing his knees up as thrower kicks him up and back.

C—Tumbler throws his head back, completing somersault.

<u>Learning Procedure</u>

(1) Tumbler performs slowly a Backward Limberover over Feet and Hands (doubles)-12.

(2) Next, he throws back and performs a backward somersault. Thrower catches his shoulders this time.

(3) Finally, he performs stunt without hand support by thrower.

<u>Spotting Technique</u>

Man on left grasps tumbler's upper arm with both hands with thumbs down.

(U-T) 25. Ankle Pick-Up Forward

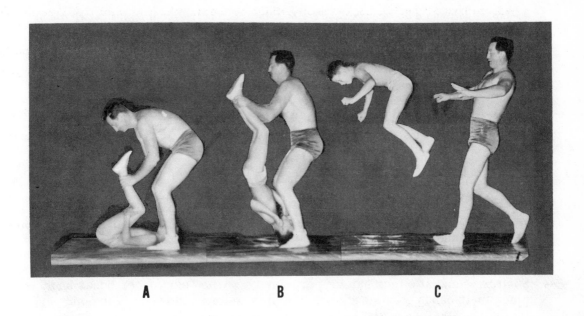

A   B   C

A—Tumbler lies down with legs bent and grasps his own legs behind knees. Thrower bends over and grasps his ankles.

B—When both are ready, thrower forcefully lifts tumbler upward off mat. Tumbler releases his grasp on his legs.

C—Thrower pushes tumbler out and snaps him down, helping him complete turn.

Thrower must be either extremely strong or use a lightweight performer.

<u>Spotting Technique</u>

Spotters stand on either side of tumbler. As thrower picks tumbler up, spotters grasp his arms and support him through turn. Even after this stunt has been learned, a spotter should kneel by performer and be ready to catch him if he does not finish stunt properly.

(L-T) 26. Double Backbends

A   B   C

A—No. 1 performs a Backbend-23, page 46. No. 2 stands, straddling his head. He bends forward and grasps No. 1 around waist, placing his head between his legs.

With knees bent he lifts No. 1 into an inverted position. No. 1 grasps No. 2 around waist.

B—No. 2 bends back while No. 1 places his feet down directly under his shoulders.

C—No. 1 leans back and with bent knees, lifts No. 2 into an inverted position. No. 1 is now ready for a Backbend.

The alternating Backbends and lifts should be done smoothly and continuously.

Performers should have good back flexibility, but they should also be strong enough to lift each other.

Learning Procedure

At first this stunt should be performed slowly. When more skill is developed, speed of performance can be increased.

Spotting Technique

Spotters stand at either side of performers. When performer bends back, spotters place their hands on his back enabling him to lower slowly. When one performer lifts the other, spotters assist him.

(L-T) 27. Forward and Backward Rolls Combined

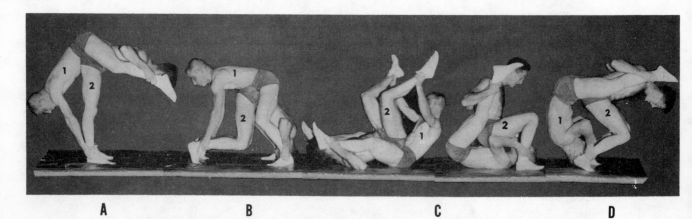

A   B   C   D

A—No. 1 lies down on his front with his legs apart. No. 2 stands facing in opposite direction between No. 1's legs. He grasps No. 1's ankles and lifts him so his hips are tightly against his lower back. He leans forward lifting No. 1 from mat. No. 1 grasps his ankles.

B—No. 2 leans forward, bends his knees and places back of his head on mat.

C—No. 1 sits down and pulls No. 2 over placing his feet down and straddling his head.

D—No. 2 completes forward roll and lifts No. 1 off mat. They are ready for another roll.

Rolls should be done continuously.

After No. 2 has rolled forward, he should bridge No. 1 to avoid sitting on him.

No. 1 and No. 2 can change positions before start of stunt putting them in position for No. 1 to roll forward and No. 2 to roll backward. Once they start, they cannot change positions.

Spotting Technique

As performer gets ready to roll forward, spotter at his right places his right hand on back of his head, helping him to duck his head.

(U-B)   28.   Low Arm-to-Arm Shoulderstand

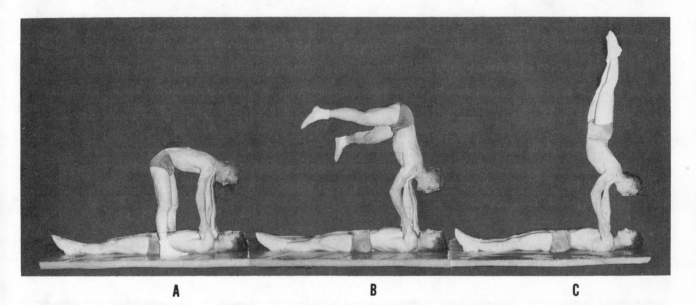

A   B   C

A—Bottom man lies down with legs together and arms raised up. Top man stands straddling bottom man with shoulders resting on bottom man's hands. He grasps outside of his upper arms.

B—With head up top man presses or kicks into balance. Bottom man locks elbows, providing him with steady support.

C—Balance is held similar to Headstand-5 (singles).

Methods of Recovery

    (1) Lower back to starting position.

    (2) Bottom man raises legs to L position. Top man lowers his. Bottom man places his feet against his groin and lowers him to stand.

    (3) Bottom man bends arms slowly, lowering top man to mat. As top man reaches mat, he ducks head and rolls forward to his back, retaining his grasp on bottom man's arms. Performers are ready for Backward Roll into Low Arm-to-Arm-28b.

Spotting Technique

Spot the same way as for Handstand-16 (singles).

a. Groin Pitch into Low Arm-to-Arm Shoulderstand

A   B   C

A—Bottom man lies down. As top man bends over him, bottom man grasps his shoulders and places his feet against his groin. Top man grasps his arms.

B—Top man leans forward as bottom man kicks him upward.

C—Bottom man supports him as he rides into Low Arm-to-Arm. Bottom man's arms are straight.

Same recovery methods as described for Low Arm-to-Arm Shoulderstand.

Spotting technique is same as for Handstand (singles).

b. Backward Roll into Low Arm-to-Arm Shoulderstand

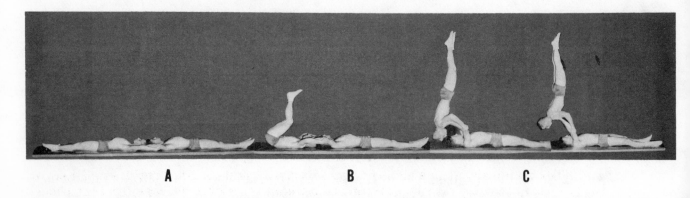

A   B   C

A—Both men lie down with their heads touching. Bottom man reaches overhead and grasps top man by shoulders. Top man grasps bottom man's upper arms on outside.

B—Top man rolls backward, kicking his legs upward and straightening his hips.

C—With straight arms, bottom man pulls him into balance. Top man keeps his body firm and his back arched during pull upward and during balance.

Use the same recovery methods described for Low Arm-to-Arm Shoulderstand.

Spotting technique is same as for Handstand-16.

(U-B) 29. Shoulderstand on Feet

A   B   C

A—Bottom man lies down with legs bent up to chest and with upper arms on mat and hands on legs behind knees. (His hips must be flat on mat and his elbows out to keep him from rolling from side to side.)

Top man places shoulders on bottom man's feet and hands on back of his thighs with thumbs in.

B —Top man kicks or presses into shoulder balance with head up. (Beginners may use this position as a stunt.)

C—Bottom man takes his hands from his legs and places them flat on mat. He slowly straightens his legs as top man slides his hands up his legs.

Methods of Recovery

(1) Lower to stand.

(2) Bottom man carries his bent legs forward and raises his straight arms upward. He grasps top man by upper arms and slowly removes his legs from his shoulders. Top man grasps his upper arms on outside. Recovery is same as described for Low Arm-to-Arm Balance and variations-28 (doubles).

Spotting Technique

Spot as for other balances.

(U-T) 30. Shoulderspring off Feet

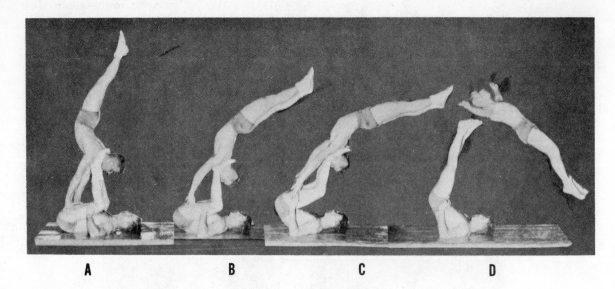

A   B   C   D

A—Tumbler performs a Shoulder Balance on Feet–29.

B—Thrower bends his knees.

C—Tumbler takes his hands off thrower's legs and overbalances.

D—Thrower kicks upward, lifting his back off mat. Tumbler completes spring, landing erect with knees bent.

Learning Procedure and Spotting Technique

Tumbler bridges over slowly to a stand without help from thrower. Spotters on either side support him by grasping his arms. As tumbler develops more skill thrower can kick him upward with spotting.

Spot as you would the Forward Somersault by Arm Lift–43. See picture on page 126 which shows technique.

(U-B) 31. Shoulder Mount from Side

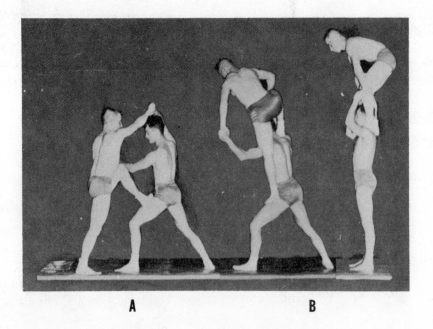

A   B

A—Bottom man stands with left leg ahead of right and with arms raised overhead and palms up. Top man places his left foot on bottom man's thigh. He grasps bottom man's hands with his thumbs in. Bottom man's first and second fingers straddle his wrist.

B —Mount is done in two ways:

(1) Top man jumps from mat, assisted by a lift from bottom man, to a stand with right foot on bottom man's shoulder. He brings left foot up later.

(2) Bottom man presses him to a stand. Top man's knees are bent up during press.

Top man straightens body and knees and raises arms sideward. Bottom man releases top man's hands one by one and places his on back of top man's legs just above calves. He pulls down on top man's legs to help him maintain balance. See picture F of Shoulder Mount from Front-39.

Bottom man reaches up with one arm at a time and regrasps top man's hands as before.

Methods of Recovery

(1) Bottom man lifts top man off shoulders and slowly lowers him forward to mat.

(2) Bending his knees, bottom man lifts top man off shoulders and lowers him backward to mat.

(3) Do a Forward Somersault off Shoulders-45.

Spotting Technique

Spotter stands at left side of top man and grasps his left upper arm with both hands. As bottom man lifts him upward, spotter also lifts. This spotter stands behind, while a second spotter stands in front.

(U-T) 32. Backward Somersault from Seat on Arms

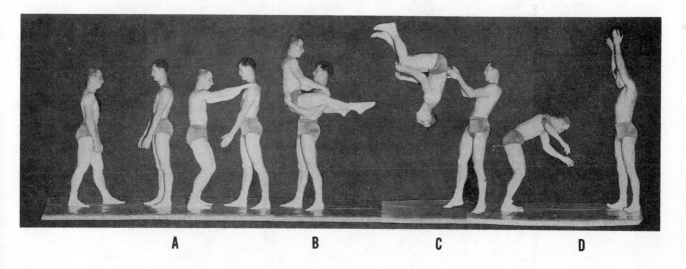

A—Tumbler walks forward and places his hands on thrower's shoulders.

B —He jumps upward bending at hips and straddling legs. Thrower reaches under and places his arms on back of tumbler's legs and his hands on his back.

C—Thrower bends his knees slightly and then straightens them, pitching tumbler over through somersault as he leans back.

D—Tumbler lands with knees bent to absorb shock of landing.

Spotting Technique

When tumbler gets to a seat on thrower's arms, spotters step in and grasp his upper arms as for Backward Somersault over feet and hands-24 (doubles). Spot in the same way.

117

(U-B) 33. Handstand

    a. On Belly

    A A   B

A—Bottom man performs a Highbridge-2b (preliminary stunt). Top man stands at his side and places his hands on his abdominal region.

B—He first pushes down on bottom man and then kicks or presses into a Handstand-16 (singles).

    b. On Back

Bottom man stands with legs straddled. He bends over with head up and places his hands above his knees with arms straight. Top man stands at bottom man's side and places his hands on his back.

He kicks or presses into a Handstand.

    c. On Hips

Bottom man bends forward, grasps back of thighs and pulls chest to thighs. Top man stands behind bottom man and places hands on bottom man's hips.

He kicks or presses into a Handstand.

    d. On Shoulders (bottom man sitting)

Bottom man sits down with straight legs, placing his straight arms back with thumbs turned out. Top man stands behind bottom man and places his hands on bottom man's shoulders.

He kicks or presses into a Handstand.

(L-T) 34. Double Cartwheels

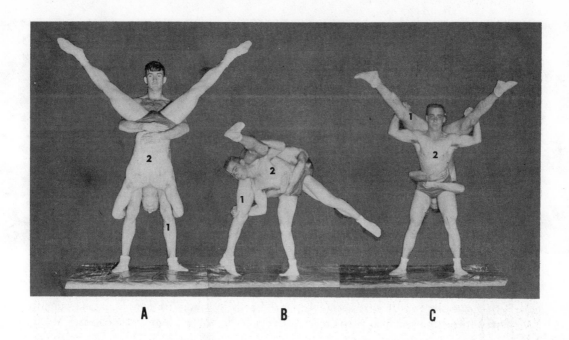

A   B   C

A—No. 2 performs a Handstand. No. 1 gets behind him, wraps his arms around No. 2's waist and lifts him off mat. No. 2 reaches back and grasps No. 1 behind knees.

B—Both men bend sideward. No. 2 places his bent right leg down. No. 1 pushes off with left foot and No. 2 straightens up, placing left foot down.

C—They have reversed positions and are ready for another Cartwheel-3 (singles). They continue stunt continuously and sideward down mat.

(U-B) 35. Double Elbow Lever

a. On Belly

Bottom man does a Highbridge-2b (preliminary stunt). Top man stands at his side and places his hands with thumbs turned out on his abdominal region.

He presses into a Double Elbow Lever-33 (singles).

He can also perform a Single Elbow Lever-33a and also a Front Planche-47 (singles).

b. On Back

Bottom and top men take positions as described for Handstand on Back-33b (doubles).

Top man presses into a Double Elbow Lever-33 (singles).

Top man can also perform a Single Elbow Lever-33a and also a Front Planche-47 (singles).

c. On Hips

Bottom and top men take positions as described for Handstand on Hips-33c (doubles).

Top man presses into a Double Elbow Lever-33 (singles).

Top man can also perform a Single Elbow Lever-33a and also a Front Planche-47 (singles).

(U-B) 36. Back Lever on Thighs

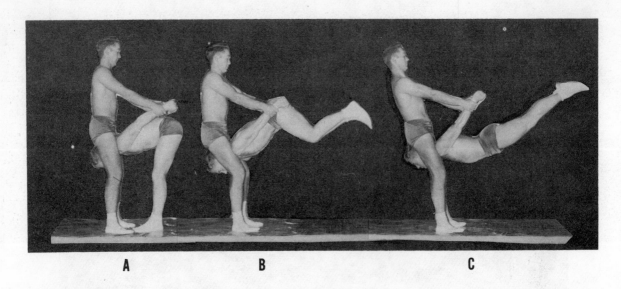

A   B   C

A—Bottom man stands with legs apart. Top man bends forward with arms back and palms in. He places head between bottom man's legs and shoulders on his thighs. Bottom man grasps him by wrists.

B—As top man raises his legs, bottom man leans backward, counterbalancing his weight.

C—Top man straightens his legs and arches his back. Both keep their arms straight.

(U-T) 37. Forward Handspring by Ankle Pitch

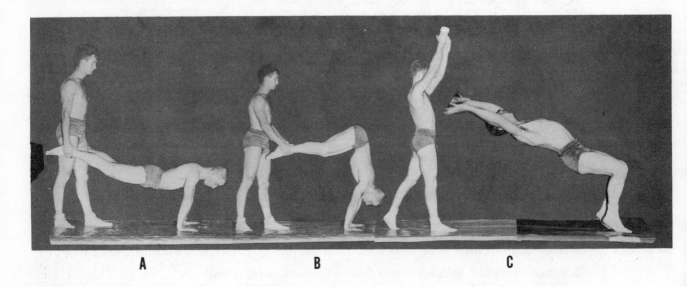

A   B   C

A—Tumbler gets into a front support with legs spread. Thrower steps between tumbler's legs and grasps his ankles.

B—As thrower lifts tumbler's legs, tumbler lifts his hips and pushes his shoulders forward.

C—Thrower leans forward and pushes tumbler through a Forward Handspring-38 (singles).

Stunt is done in one motion.

Spotting Technique

Use the same spotting technique as for the Forward Handspring.

(L-T) 38. Forward Handspring by Neck Lift

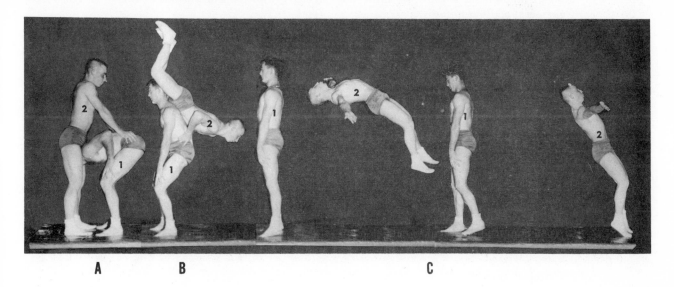

A   B   C

A—No. 1 bends forward, placing his head between No. 2's legs and his hands on his thighs. With thumbs in, No. 2 places his hands on No. 1's hips.

B —No. 1 raises his body forcefully.

C—Just before No. 1 reaches an upright position, No. 2 pushes off and does a Handspring.

Learning Procedure and Spotting Technique

(1) Spotters stand on either side of tumbler and grasp his arm as for Forward Handspring-38. Thrower lifts slowly and tumbler bridges over to a stand with help from spotters.

(2) Performers do stunt faster with assistance.

(U-B) 39. Shoulder Mount from Front

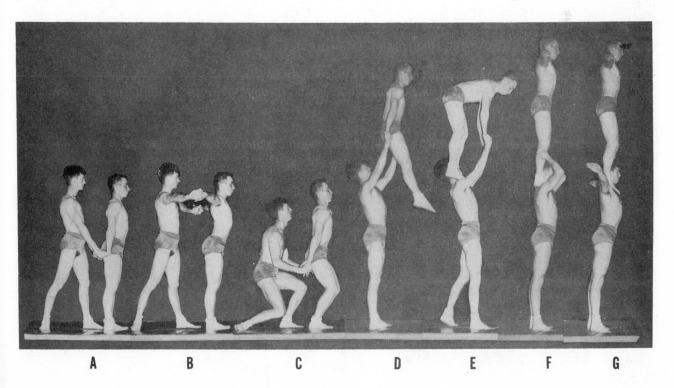

A   B   C   D   E   F   G

A—Bottom man takes a stride stand with left leg forward. Top man stands in front of him with hands hanging down and thumbs turned in. Bottom man grasps top man's hands with his first and second fingers straddling his wrist.

B—Both performers swing their arms sideward then downward.

C—Bottom man bends his knees deeply, gets under top man and lifts him overhead.

D—Top man helps by springing upward with knees raised as bottom man lifts him upward. At peak of lift bottom man bends his wrists back.

E—Bottom man slowly lowers top man to a stand on his shoulders.

F—Top man straightens up as bottom man grasps his legs. This is described under Shoulder Mount from Side-31 (doubles).

G—Both men raise their arms sideward and hold a free balance. Bottom man regrasps top man's hands.

The only way for top man to dismount from bottom man's shoulders is while both have their hands clasped.

Learning Procedure

(1) Up and Down. Bottom man lifts top man as in picture D and then lowers him to mat. He does this over and over until a coordinated jump and lift between them are obtained.

(2) Mount to Seat on Shoulders. Top man jumps and bottom man lifts him to a seat on his shoulders instead of to a stand.

Methods of Recovery

Use recovery methods on page 117 for Shoulder Mount from Side-31. Another method is to have bottom man slowly lower top man to where he is in a Front Angel Straddling Waist-4. Without pausing top man rolls forward and bottom man lowers him controlled to mat.

This is the reverse of Backward Roll, Mount to Shoulders-40.

Spotting Technique

Performers stand as described above. Spotters stand in front of and to side of top man and grasp his arms. As bottom man lifts and top man jumps, spotters lift top man upward. They retain their grasp until top man is secure on bottom man's shoulders.

When spotters do not assist bottom man in lifting top man to his shoulders, they stand one in front and one in back of bottom man with arms raised overhead. In this position, they are ready to assist the top man if he loses his balance while standing on bottom man's shoulders.

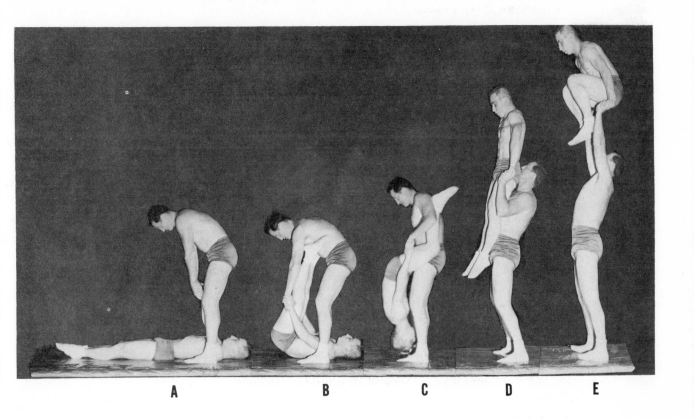

A—Top man lies down with arms raised. Bottom man straddles him and grasps his hands as for Shoulder Mount from Front-39.

B—Top man raises his legs and starts his roll backward.

C—Bottom man lifts top man from floor as he straddles his waist. Top man rolls to an upright position, keeping close to bottom man.

D—Bottom man bends his wrist back sharply and presses top man upward, forcefully straightening his arms.

E—Top man places his feet on bottom man's shoulders. Bottom man grasps behind his knees.

Learning Procedure

An easier version is to do a Backward Roll to a Seat on Shoulders. This requires less strength than a lift to a stand.

Methods of Recovery

See recovery methods for Shoulder Mount from Front-39. They apply to this stunt as well.

The spotting technique is the same as for Shoulder Mount from Front.

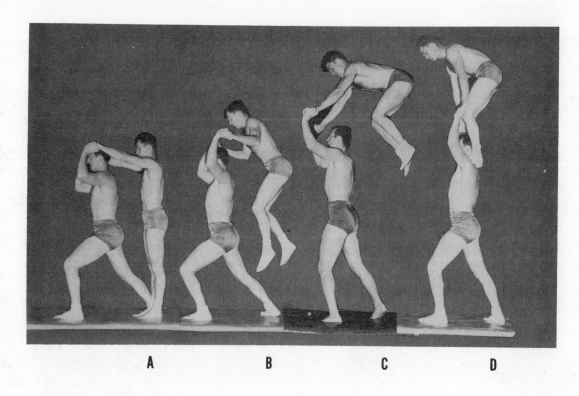

A   B   C   D

A—Bottom man stands in a stride position with left knee bent and arms raised overhead. Top man stands behind him, reaches up and grasps his hands.

B —Both men bend their knees. Then top man jumps, putting his weight on bottom man's hands.

C—At same time, bottom man straightens his arms and legs and pulls top man overhead. As he does this, he leans forward, putting his weight over his left leg.

D—Top man lands on bottom man's shoulders. Bottom man grasps his legs behind knees. Bottom man releases hold on legs and grasps top man's hands. Then top man dismounts.

Methods of Recovery

Use recovery methods listed under Shoulder Mounts from Side-31, from Front-39 and from Backward Roll-40. In addition do the ones listed below:

(1) Top man jumps backward, landing about six inches from bottom man. As he lands, he immediately jumps upward again. Bottom man lifts and pulls him back to stand.

Top man must be careful not to land on bottom man's right ankle when he jumps backward.

Bottom man must bend his knees and arms as top man lands to avoid straining his back and shoulders.

(2) Top man can jump down and up again, doing a Forward Somersault by Arm Lift-43.

Since the above recovery methods are quite difficult, they were explained along with the more difficult stunts in hopes their learning will be postponed.

Spotting Technique

Spotters stand behind and to side of bottom man. They grasp top man's upper arms with both hands and help him up to bottom man's shoulders. While he is standing on bottom man's shoulders, they keep their arms up, ready to catch him if he should lose his balance.

(U-B) 42. Shoulder Mount by Three Jumps

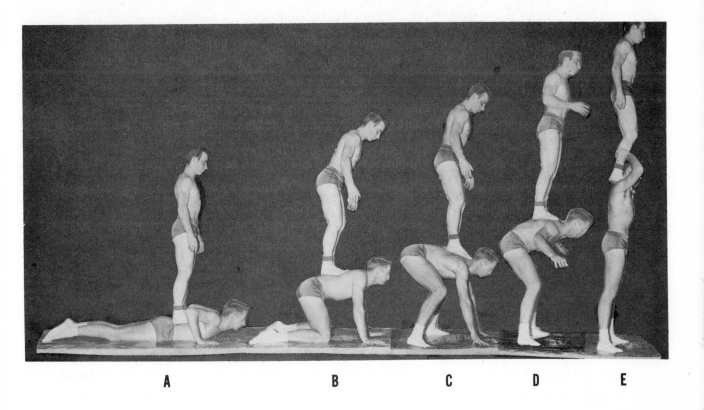

A   B   C   D   E

A—Bottom man lies down. Top man stands on his back. Bottom man places his hands by his side and prepares to lift his body.

B—Top man signals and jumps upward. He is followed immediately by bottom man who straightens his arms and jumps to his knees. Top man lands on bottom man's back.

C—Top man takes his second jump, landing high on bottom man's back after bottom man jumps to his feet.

D—Bottom man raises his hands from mat.

E—Bottom man straightens up and grasps top man's calves after top man has taken his third jump and landed on bottom man's shoulders.

Methods of Recovery

Both men lean and start to fall forward. Then top man jumps and performs a Forward Roll. Bottom man also does one at the same time. See also Shoulder Mount from Side-31 (doubles), Shoulder Mount from Front-39 and Shoulder Mount from Back-41 for additional recoveries.

Spotting Technique

The spotting technique is the same as for Shoulder Mount from Front (doubles) after the top man has gotten to the shoulders of bottom man after three jumps. During rise to stand, spotters should stand on either side of performers ready to catch top man if he should lose his balance.

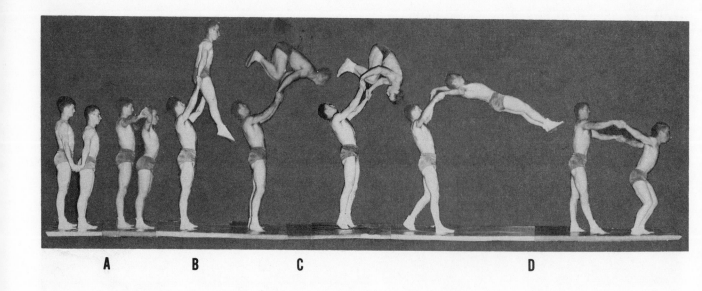

A   B   C   D

A—Performers take positions described under Shoulder Mount from Front-39.

B —Bottom man lifts top man upward as if for a shoulder mount.

C—At peak of lift, top man in a tucked position turns over forward while bottom man supports him.

D—Bottom man holds top man's hands until he lands.

 Top man must keep his legs in close to chest to keep from kicking the bottom man.

Spotting Technique

Spotter on left grasps top man's upper arm with left hand high and right low, thumbs down. Spotter on other side does opposite. In this way they can support tumbler while he turns over forward.

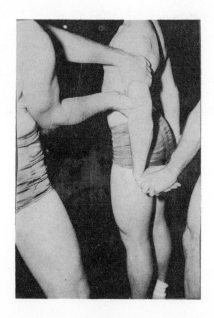

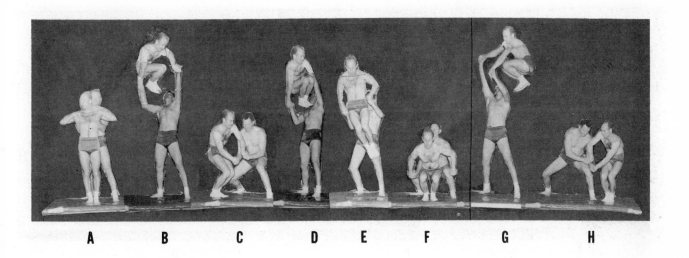

A—Performers take a stand for a Shoulder Mount from Front-39 (doubles).

B —Top man jumps upward and bottom man lifts. As top man reaches peak of his jump, he turns to left and passes over bottom man's right arm. As he jumps out bottom man swings his arm in and under top man.

C—As top man lands, bottom man bends deeply.

D—He immediately springs and bottom man lifts him upward.

E —Top man turns right and passes over bottom man's right arm. Bottom man swings his arm out and under top man's legs.

F —He controls top man's descent to mat.

G—Top man springs while bottom man lifts him upward.

H—This time he jumps out to left and springs back into center again.

Jumping in and out can be used as a recovery method from stand on shoulders.

(On jumps in and out top man keeps his knees bent deeply.)

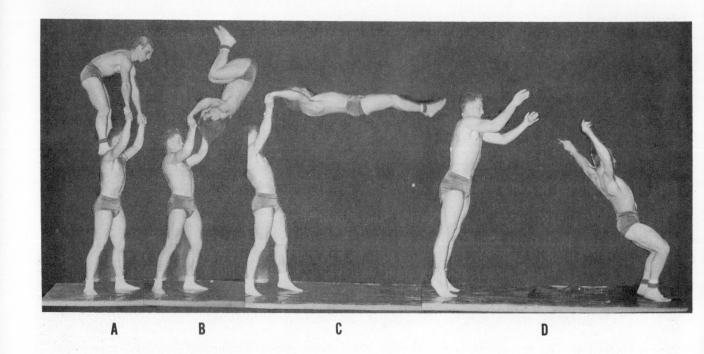

A   B   C   D

A—Top man mounts to shoulders. They retain grasp.

B —Bottom man springs off bottom man's shoulders, ducks head and tucks knees up to chest.

C—Bottom man holds arms overhead to support top man during his turn over forward.

D—Bottom man keeps arms high, enabling top man to complete somersault high above mat.

Spotting Technique

Spotters stand in front of bottom man. Here they can catch top man around waist if he does not complete somersault or if he overturns it.

(U-T) 46. Groin Pitch (Forward Handspring from Feet)

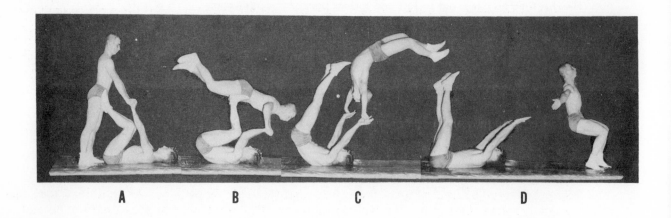

A   B   C   D

A—Thrower lies down with arms and legs raised. He places his feet, slightly turned out against tumbler's groin and grasps top man's hands. Both men have their thumbs turned in.

B —When both men are ready, tumbler leans forward, putting his weight on thrower's arms and legs.

C—Thrower bends his arms and legs deeply. Then he extends his legs and arms forcefully, pushing tumbler upward and over.

D—Tumbler pushes off with his hands and completes forward handspring.

The tumbler should have a good Forward Handspring-38 (singles) before he does this stunt.

Spotting Technique

Spotters grasp upper arms as pictured on page 126.

(U-T) 47. Forward Handspring over Head

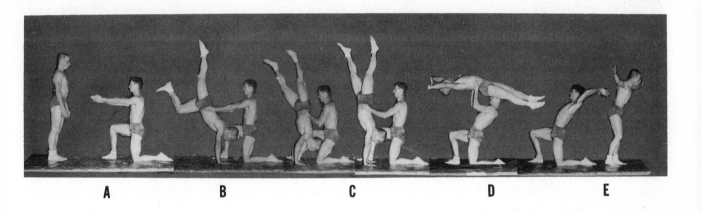

A   B   C   D   E

A—Tumbler stands facing thrower who is kneeling on left knee.

B—Tumbler kicks forcefully into a Handstand.

C—Thrower places his hands on tumbler's back and stops him before he reaches vertical position.

D—He immediately lifts tumbler upward. (He can raise him overhead while still kneeling as pictured above or he can rise to a stand while holding tumbler horizontal.)

E—Then he pushes tumbler up and over. Tumbler lands with his knees bent and with his head back to keep from overturning handspring.

Action of tumbler is fast; therefore, thrower must also act quickly in placing his hands on tumbler's back and in lifting him overhead.

Spotting Technique

Spotters assist tumbler as if for a Forward Handspring or Kip. As tumbler kicks upward, spotters help thrower lift him upward. When thrower pushes tumbler up and over, spotters release their grasp on his arms. They wait to catch him if he overturns or underturns the handspring.

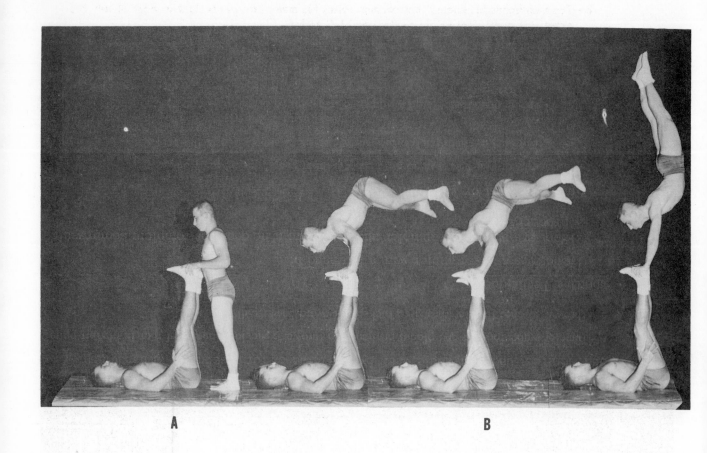

A   B

A—Bottom man lies down, placing hands on thighs with elbows out to sides resting on mat. Top man puts his hands on bottom man's feet.

B—Top man leans forward and kicks or presses into a Handstand-16 (singles).

If top man overbalances Handstand, he can do a quarter turn and land at bottom man's side.

a. Handstand on Feet (Regular), Half Turn to (Reverse) Foot-to-Hand

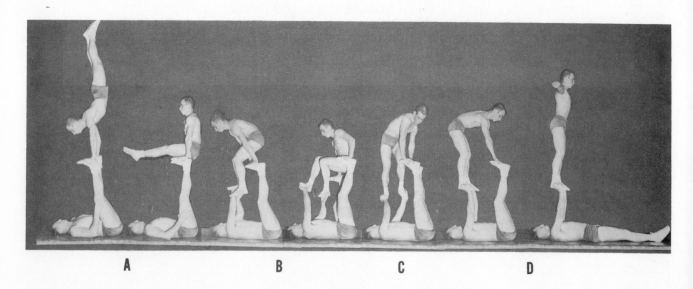

A   B   C   D

A—From a Handstand on Feet top man slowly lowers his legs and then raises them to an L position.

B—Top man bends his knees. Bottom man raises his arms, crosses his right in front of left and grasps top man's feet—right to right and left to left.

C—Top man pushes off.

D—Bottom man twists him around until both are in a regular Foot-to-Hand-14 (doubles). Bottom man lowers legs to mat.

Spotting Technique

Spotters stand at sides of top man and keep their hands up. If top man should lose his balance, he can grasp spotters' hands.

(U-T) 49. Backward Somersault from Lying Pitch

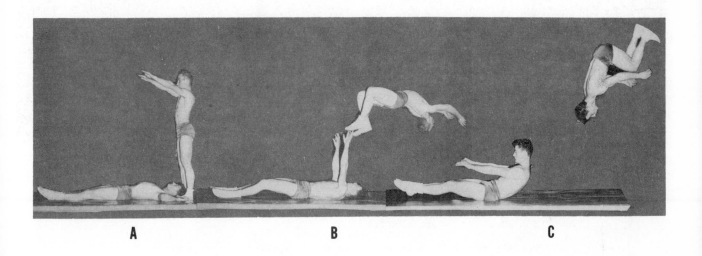

A   B   C

A—Thrower lies down fully extended with bent arms raised overhead and with palms up. Tumbler stands on thrower's hands facing him. Thrower grasps his feet.

B—When both are ready, tumbler throws a Backward Somersault-45 (singles) assisted by a lift from thrower.

C—After lifting, thrower sits up.

The head is the controlling factor in turning over, therefore, the longer the tumbler delays throwing his head backward on the take-off, the higher will be his somersault. However, if he waits too long, he will have difficulty in turning the somersault. He must, through practice, discover the right time to throw his head.

Spotting Technique

Spot as for Backward Somersault.

(U-T) 50. Backward Somersault from Sitting Pitch

A   B   C

A—Thrower sits down with legs apart and with back of hands on mat. Tumbler steps on thrower's hands, who grasps his feet.

B —Tumbler swings his arms downward and backward as he bends his knees.

C—He swings his arms upward and overhead and jumps as thrower pitches him through a Backward Somersault–45 (singles).

Spotting Technique

Spot the same as for the Backward Somersault.

(U-T) 51. Backward Somersault by Leg Pitch

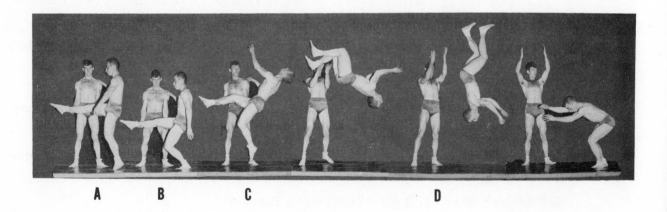

A   B   C   D

A—Thrower stands on side of mat with elbows bent and palms up. Tumbler stands at thrower's left side about three feet away. He takes three steps forward, starting and ending on left foot. He raises straight right leg upward. Thrower grasps it with right hand on calf and left on back of thigh. Tumbler places right hand on thrower's left shoulder.

B —Thrower bends both legs. Tumbler bends his left knee and presses down with his right leg against thrower's hands.

C—Thrower straightens up and forcefully lifts tumbler's straight right leg. Tumbler pushes off thrower's shoulder with hand and off mat with left foot.

D—He throws his arms over and his head back and completes somersault.

Thrower keeps his hands up ready to assist tumbler if he should underturn somersault.

Remember—Don't throw head too soon. This cuts the height of somersault.

Don't throw head too late. This stalls the somersault.

Don't try this stunt until you can perform a Backward Somersault (Standing).

Spotting Technique

(1) Spot as for Backward Somersault over Feet and Hands-24 (doubles).

(2) Use flat hand belt. For technique see page 2 under Spotting Technique-2, Hand-Belt Spotting.

a. With Half Twist by Leg Pitch

Thrower pitches tumbler into Backward Somersault. Then tumbler does a half twist to left while completing somersault. Look under 45a Backward Somersault with Half Twist (Standing) (singles) for the technique of performing the half twist.

Do not rush twist. Lift somersault first; then twist.

Spotting Technique

(1) See page 85, Spotting Technique for Backward Somersault with Half Twist-45a (singles).

If tumbler twists to left, spotter should stand at his right side to keep from getting hit by his right hand. If tumbler underturns, spotter can place his right hand on his back to keep him from falling back. If tumbler overturns, spotter can place his left arm across his chest to keep him from falling forward.

(2) Use twisting hand belt. Support performer as for any other somersault.

b. With Full Twist by Leg Pitch

Thrower pitches tumbler forcefully into Backward Somersault. Then tumbler does a full twist to left while completing somersault.

Don't do this stunt until you have tried Backward Somersault with Full Twist (Standing) (singles).

Do not rush twist. Lift somersault first; then twist.

Spotting Technique

Use twisting hand belt. Spotter at left side of performer grasps rope with left hand about two feet from belt. He places his right hand about six inches from belt. Spotter at right side does just the opposite. When tumbler reaches an upside-down position, spotter on left side steps in toward performer with right foot and slides his right hand in toward him. Spotter on other side does the opposite. This puts them in position to support performer.

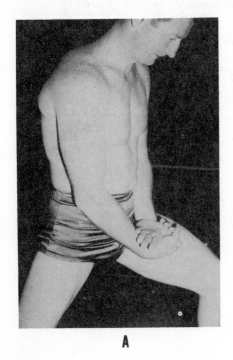

A   B   C   D

A—Thrower stands erect in a stride with left leg forward and right back. He rests back of left wrist on thigh and arms against body. Then he grasps left thumb with right hand and supports back of left on right wrist.

B—Tumbler takes three steps toward thrower starting and ending walk with left foot. When he gets within a foot of thrower, he places his hands on thrower's shoulders and his right foot in thrower's palm.

C—Tumbler pushes down with right foot and hands. Then thrower pushes against his foot and lifts him upward.

D—Tumbler pushes off with his hands and his foot and springs over thrower's head with his legs straddled. He lands behind thrower with knees bent.

Spotting Technique

Spotters stand just behind thrower ready to catch tumbler if he looks as if he is going to land improperly.

A   B

See picture A under Straddle Vault by Toe Pitch-52 for description of handclasp.

A—Tumbler walks forward and places his hands on thrower's shoulders and right foot in his left palm.

B—Thrower pitches tumbler through a tucked Backward Somersault.

Spotting Technique

(1) Spotters assist tumbler with a flat hand belt.

(2) Spotters stand near tumbler and catch him if he does not complete somersault properly.

a. With Half Twist by Toe Pitch

See Backward Somersault with Half Twist by Leg Pitch-51a (doubles).

See also Backward Somersault with Half Twist-45a (singles) (standing).

Tumbler should pull arms close to chest to facilitate twist. He should also bring his legs together as soon as possible for best form.

b. With Full Twist by Toe Pitch

See Backward Somersault with Full Twist by Leg Pitch-51b (doubles).

See also Backward Somersault with Full Twist-45b (standing) (singles).

(U-T) 54. Forward Somersault by Foot Pitch

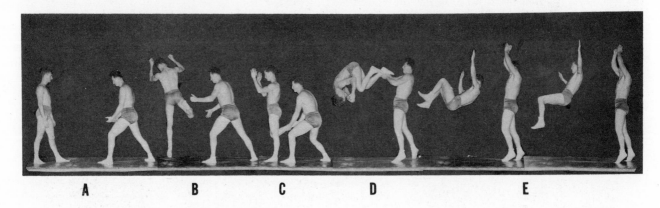

A   B   C   D   E

A—Tumbler walks forward toward thrower.

B—He ends walk with arms raised and with left leg forward. Then he hops on left foot with right leg bent, performing a half turn left.

C—Thrower grasps tumbler's foot with both hands. Tumbler pushes down on thrower's hands with right leg. Thrower lifts tumbler upward by pushing against right leg while tumbler springs off with his left.

D—At peak of lift, tumbler does somersault by ducking his head and driving his arms downward. He completes somersault by grasping his knees and pulling his legs under him.

E—He releases his grasp, landing upright with knees bent.

Spotting Technique

Spotters assist performer in the same way as for the Forward Somersault-44b (standing) (singles).

(U-B) 55. Handstand on Feet (Low), Calf Lift

A   B   C

136

A—Bottom man lies down resting on his forearms with legs apart. Top man stands facing away from and straddling bottom man. He grasps soles of bottom man's feet and kicks or presses into a Handstand-16 (singles).

B—As bottom man prepares to lift him, top man slightly underbalances his Handstand to facilitate the lift.

C—Then bottom man presses hard on his arms and lifts his legs upward to a vertical position. Top man maintains his balance.

Bottom man slowly lowers top man to starting position.

Learning Procedure

Start with a very light person and after many repetitions attempt to lift a heavier person.

(U-B)   56. Low Hand-to-Hand Handstand (Regular Grasp) (Low Hand-to-Hand)

A   B

A—Bottom man lies down with arms raised and thumbs in. Top man stands facing and straddling bottom man. He grasps bottom man's hands with thumbs in.

B—Top man kicks or presses into Handstand.

Methods of Recovery

(1) Bottom man lowers him to starting position.

(2) Bottom man raises his legs to top man's waist. Then top man lowers his body into a Front Angel Balance-1 (doubles). Bottom man grasps top man's shoulders and:

    (a) Holds him in Low Arm-to-Arm Shoulderstand-28 (doubles). See Recovery Methods under this stunt.

    (b) Pitches him over.

    (c) Bridges him over.

A—Bottom man lies down with legs raised. Top man rests his body against bottom man's feet and crosses his arms in front with right arm over left. Bottom man reaches straight up and grasps top man's hands left to left and right to right.

B—Top man leans forward as bottom man bends his knees. Bottom man pushes top man upward and straightens his arms.

C—Top man does a half turn to left into a Low Hand-to-Hand Handstand.

Methods of Recovery

    (1) Lower to Thighstand-16a.

    (2) Lower into Front Lever on Thighs-59.

    (3) Do Get-Up into High Hand-to-Hand Handstand-65.

    (4) Do French Rolls-64.

    (5) Bottom man squats his legs between his arms and top man goes to One-Handed Handstand to Single Elbow Lever-67.

A   B(1)   B(2)   C

A—Performers stand facing each other. Bottom man grasps top man by shoulders with thumbs in his armpits. Top man grasps bottom man by upper arm on outside.

B—Methods of Getting into Balance.

(1) Top man jumps and straddles bottom man with legs under his armpits. As top man straddles him, bottom man leans forward, lowering top man to within a few inches of mat. Bottom man leans backward, lifting top man overhead into a piked position.

(2) Top man jumps as bottom man lifts him overhead.

C—Bottom man straightens up. Then top man slowly raises his straight legs overhead. If top man overbalances, bottom man makes a half turn and slowly lowers him back to mat.

A   B   C   D

A—Performers do a Low Hand-to-Hand Handstand. See 57 Groin Pitch into Low Hand-to-Hand.

B—Bottom man slowly bends his arms and places his elbows on mat.

C—He bends knees, places soles of feet on mat and raises body. Top man leans forward and lowers shoulders to bottom man's knees. Bottom man pulls his hands back to counterbalance top man's weight.

D—Top man ducks his head and slowly lowers his arched body into a horizontal balance (Front Lever), lifting bottom man off mat. After holding top man in balance several seconds, bottom man lowers him to mat.

(U-B) 60. Handstand on Forearm

A   B

A—Bottom man stands with left forearm raised, with palm up and elbow against thigh bone. He braces himself as top man grasps his arm with left hand and his palm with right hand.

B—Top man kicks or presses into a Handstand-16 (singles) as bottom man leans back with his weight on his right leg. (Bottom man can place right hand on top man's knee and lift him up as he jumps.) Top man puts most of his weight on left arm to enable bottom man to more easily support him.

Top man lowers himself to mat.

$\left(U\text{-}\dfrac{T}{B}\right)$ 61. Cannonball to Flag (Foot-to-Hand), to Scale, to Back Flag (Foot-to-Hand)

A   B   C

A—Top man lies down on back and raises legs to an L position.

Bottom man stands facing top man and straddles his head. Bottom man grasps soles of other's feet. He snaps him through a Backward Roll and he does a quarter turn left, straightening body. He lowers right arm to thigh and holds top man in a Flag.

B—Bottom man pulls top man up by left leg while lifting right forearm to waist level. He releases other man's left leg and when he is balanced, he raises left leg back to a Front Scale, page 23.

C—Top man lowers arms and left leg and straightens up. Bottom man regrasps top man's foot with fingers over instep. He bends knees and lowers right arm until it rests on thigh. He leans back while he lowers top man backward into a Back Flag.

He lowers top man farther and top man places hands down. He releases grasp and top man does a Backward Walkover-25 (singles).

(U-B) 62. Flag (Hand-to-Hand)

Bottom man stands straddled with knees bent and with back of left hand resting on his thigh. Top man stands at bottom man's left side and grasps bottom man's left hand with his left. He reaches across with right and grasps bottom man's right hand. Bottom leans right sideward and pulls top man off mat with right arm. Top man turns so his left side is toward mat. He locks out his left arm and tightens his body to do a Side Planche-49.

(See Bert Goodrich and George Redpath in a classic pose opposite.)

Method of Recovery

Bottom man lowers top man to mat.

Learning Procedure

Bottom man squats with his left leg forward and back of his left hand resting on his left thigh just above knee. Top man leans over sideward and grasps bottom man's left hand with his left. He reaches over with right hand thumb down and grasps bottom man's right hand. Bottom man leans back slowly and raises top man slowly off mat into a Flag.

Stand with right side near a set of parallettes (very low parallel bars). Bend over and place left hand on mat and right on left bar. Kick into Handstand-16 and slowly lower sideward into Side Planche.

(U-B) 63. Get-Up from Low to High Cheststand

A B C D

A—Bottom man lies down with right leg bent back and with right arm up and left arm sideward. Top man leans over bottom man and grasps his right arm with his left hand high and his right low. Bottom man spreads his fingers and places his hand against top man's chest.

B—Bottom man turns to left putting all his weight on left side. He leans forward, pushes with left hand and rises to a sitting position, bringing left leg back under hips.

C—He pushes off with left hand and rises to a kneeling position.

D—He steps forward with right foot and rises to a stride stand. Slowly he slides left foot forward closer to right.

Methods of Recovery

(1) Bottom man reverses procedure and lowers himself back down to mat.

(2) Top man can release his grasp on bottom man's arm and jump down to mat behind him.

Learning Procedure

Start with a light person and finally build up to a heavier one.

(U-B) 64. French Rolls (Barrel Rolls) (Elbow Rolls) in Low Hand-to-Hand Handstand

A—Top man kicks or presses into a Low Hand-to-Hand Handstand with hands reversed. See picture C of Groin Pitch into Low Hand-to-Hand Handstand-57.

B—Bottom man slowly lowers his right arm sideward to mat while top man bends left arm.

C—Bottom man crosses left leg over right, slides right arm up and raises left shoulder off mat.

D—He continues roll until he has left elbow down on mat. Top man straightens his left arm.

E—Bottom man continues turn to right by lifting his right arm and by turning his head to right. Top man bends right arm. Bottom man lowers his right elbow to mat and slides his left arm to his side while he brings his right leg around. Top man straightens right arm.

F—He presses top man into a Low Hand-to-Hand Handstand.

The Recovery Method is the same as for Groin Pitch into Low Hand-to-Hand Handstand-57.

a. French Rolls in Foot-to-Hand Stand

The technique of performing this stunt is the same as for the French Rolls in a Low Hand-to-Hand Handstand on the preceding pages. See Foot-to-Hand Stand-14 (doubles).

(U-B) 65. Get-Up from Low to High Hand-to-Hand Handstand

A—Performers do a Low Hand-to-Hand Handstand reversed. (See picture C Groin Pitch into Low Hand-to-Hand-57.)

B—Top man slightly overbalances as bottom man slowly rises to a sitting position with arms bent.

C—He prepares to get to his knees by bringing right leg back then left.

D—He leans forward and rises to a kneel.

E—He steps forward on left foot.

F—He leans forward and rises to a stand.

G—Finally, he sets himself and pushes top man into a High Hander.

Method of Recovery

(1) Do reverse of this stunt and return to a Low Hand-to-Hand.

(2) Bottom man lowers top man to a tucked position between his legs as in pictures E, D, C, in that order, of Cannonball to Handstand-68 (doubles). Then he snaps him up again to a Handstand as described for Cannonball to Handstand.

(U-B) 66. Low One Hand-to-Hand Handstand

A B

A—Bottom man lies down with arms and right leg up. He bends left leg and places foot firmly on mat. Top man stands at bottom man's right side and places his left hand on his left. Bottom man grasps it. Then he grasps his wrist with right hand.

Top man kicks or presses into a Handstand with right arm bent.

B —Top man shifts weight over his left shoulder and releases his grasp on bottom man's right foot to perform a One-Handed Handstand. See singles tumbling stunt 16p.

Methods of Recovery

Top man performs a quarter turn clockwise and grasps bottom man's right hand to perform a Low Hand-to-Hand Handstand.

(U-B) 67. Low Hand-to-Hand Handstand, to Low One-Handed Handstand, to Single Elbow Lever

A B C D

A—Performers do a Low Hand-to-Hand Handstand reversed.

B —Bottom man slowly lowers elbows to mat. He brings legs up with knees bent between arms to a Pretzel Bend position. (See preliminary stunt-1.)

C—He straightens knees. Top man stretches body, leans to left and performs a One-Handed Handstand. (See singles stunt-16p.) He leans back to right and regrasps bottom man's right hand. Bottom man rests hands against back. Top man lowers to Double Elbow Lever-33 singles.

D—He leans right and does a Single Elbow Lever-33a. Bottom man tilts head to right and rolls over right shoulder like Fishflop-31b singles, Method Two.

$\left(U\text{-}\dfrac{T}{B}\right)$ 68. Cannonball to High Hand-to-Hand Handstand

A   B C D E

A—With right leg forward, bottom man squats behind top man and grasps his hands. Both men have thumbs in.

B—Bottom man quickly steps forward with left foot and brings his right foot even with his left. This leaves him crouched over top man with bent arms. At same time, top man bends his arms and brings his knees up to his chest.

C—Thrower snaps his straight arms up to a horizontal position, lifting tumbler off mat in a tuck.

D—He continues lift without pause by bringing his lower arms close to body and by bending his wrists back.

E—He presses top man into a High Hand-to-Hand Handstand.

Methods of Recovery

(1) Top man lowers his legs between his arms to an L position. Then bottom man lowers him forward to a stand.

(2) Bottom man lowers top man to a Low Hand-to-Hand Handstand by doing reverse of Get-Up from Low to High Hand-to-Hand Handstand.

a. High One Hand-to-Hand Handstand (bottom man's arm bent)

A   B   C

A—Performers do a Cannonball to a High Hand-to-Hand Handstand. See opposite page.

B —Bottom man bends his arms and lowers top man to a bent arm High Hand-to-Hand Handstand.
   Then he lowers his right arm a little to help top man get into position for his one-armer.

C—Top man shifts his weight over right arm and slowly raises his left arm sideward into a One Arm
   Handstand. See 16p (singles).

Methods of Recovery

Bottom man regrasps top man's left hand and presses him into a High Hand-to-Hand
with straight arms.

In handbalancing the bottom man must be strong and reasonably flexible; the top
man an exceptional balancer with excellent form and style of performance.

Advanced doubles balancing is a fine art requiring many years of patient practice.
This art, correctly executed, is a thrill to observe.

Chapter 4

Pyramid Building

Pyramid building in gymnastics is architecture of sinew instead of steel. It has fascinated people of all ages; it is still a fascinating activity. Boys and girls at all levels of ability can participate with satisfaction.

Pyramid building is guided by art and scientific principles. Guiding art principles are beauty, symmetry, simplicity of design and power; guiding scientific principles are solidness of foundation, center of gravity and balance.

<u>Beauty</u> shows up in the neatness and appearance of the performers and performance, and in the colorfulness of costumes.

<u>Symmetry</u> is practiced by using like individuals and groups in similar positions.

<u>Simplicity</u> shows up in designs easily comprehended; not in designs where arms and legs are intertwined unintelligibly.

<u>Power</u> is displayed by the bottom men, as the bases, supporting the top men.

<u>Solidness of foundation</u> is obviously shown by the ease with which performers move into their positions and the control displayed when the pyramid is finally completed.

<u>Center of gravity</u> is observed by equal distribution of weight around the center of the pyramid.

<u>Balance</u> is achieved by poses at one end duplicated by poses at the opposite end and by equal spacing between poses.

Pyramids can start with three, four or five people holding a pose dependent one on another and progress to where related groups of fifty or more can construct one pyramid.

The progressive development of pyramids takes the form of arithmetical progression. If three people do the same trick, like a Headstand, in a single file, this could be expressed: one, one, one. If four people composed a pyramid of a Headstand at either end and a doubles balancing stunt in the middle, this would be: one, two, one. Next a triples stunt could be done flanked by singles balances: one, three, one, and so forth.

The next step, to avoid getting too high in the middle, would be three doubles balances in a single file: two, two, two. Next would be: two, three, two.

Another step would be singles and doubles stunts, flanking a triples balance in the middle: one, two, three, two, one. This procedure could go on ad infinitum. Remember: It is easier to expand sideward than to keep climbing higher; however, a combination pose of four or five men can be developed as the middle part of the pyramid progressing outward to either side: one, two, three, four, three, two, one, or one, two, three, four, five, four, three, two, one. The doubles and triples balances in the middle depend on the strength of the bottom performers and the agility and ability of the top performers. Because of safety and appearance, it is foolhardy to try to build pyramids which are too difficult.

Pyramids can be composed of separate groups of individuals or individuals who connect into a total pyramid. There are several types: straight line, curved line, tower and intersecting lines. A straight-line pyramid is one which extends sideward with performers facing forward and/or sideward. Four straight-line pyramids can be joined to form a square or diamond.

Curved pyramids are similar to the straight line except they take a concave appearance.

The tower pyramid can have a round or square base and it resembles a tower, or spire. It is pictured below.

Intersecting-line pyramids are ones in which two-line pyramids cross and build to a high point at the center. These are usually viewed by an audience surrounding or viewing the performance from above. An example is pictured below.

Tower Pyramid   Intersecting-Line Pyramid

There are five basic body positions that performers can assume at any of the three levels: sitting, hands and knees, lying, kneeling and standing. In addition to these the individual balancing stunts covered in Chapter 2 can be used.

Pyramids can usually rise to three levels at the center; however, the three-high position is difficult to achieve. Care must be taken in getting the performer up to the high perch and down again. Experienced performers are needed as well as experienced spotters, who should stand at the front and back ready to catch the performer if he should slip.

Spot balances in the pyramids as described for the Headstand-5 (singles); spot shoulder mounts and similar stunts as described for Mount to Shoulders from Side-31 (doubles). Use a table, ladder or anything sturdy to reach a performer who is two or three high. There should be two spotters in front and two in back.

TRIPLES PYRAMIDS

The following three pyramids show a progression in difficulty, outside performers go from a horizontal to a vertical position. The middle performer supports outer performers. Performers stand single file, facing forward.

1. Numbers 1 and 2 step forward and get in a push-up position-1 (strength stunt), facing sideward. Number 3 stands between with arms obliquely downward.

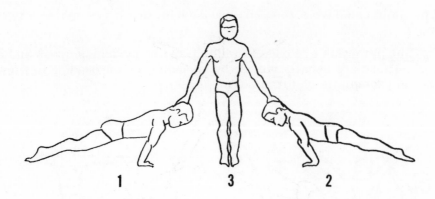

Same starting position and after performance, all return to single file in all pyramid work.

2. Numbers 1 and 2 get in a push-up position, facing sideward and away from each other. Number 3 stands between them. He grasps Number 2's inside ankle with left hand and lifts him diagonally upward, shifting hand so palm is up. He grasps Number 1's ankle and lifts him upward.

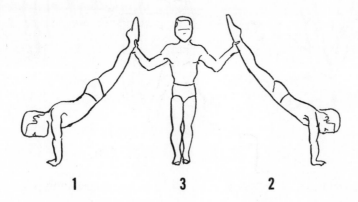

3. Number 1 kicks up and Number 3 places right hand between Number 1's feet and grasps his forward ankle. Number 2 kicks up from opposite side and Number 3 grasps his ankle.

The following six pyramids show a performer supported by two bottom men. They show the various positions bottom men can assume. The pyramids progress in difficulty.

4. Numbers 1 and 2 get in a push-up position. Number 3 steps up and stands on the backs of their necks.

5. Numbers 1 and 2 get on hands and knees. Number 3 steps up and stands on the backs of their necks.

6. Numbers 1 and 2 sit with their arms and legs extended. Number 3 steps up to a stand on their shoulders with his feet turned out.

7. Numbers 1 and 2 lie side by side with both arms raised and backs of hands on mat. Number 3 steps on their hands and they lift him.

8. Numbers 1 and 2 kneel and clasp their arms. Number 3 steps up to a stand on their shoulders.

9. Numbers 1 and 2 stand facing each other and clasp arms. Number 3 places right foot on Number 1's left hand and left foot on Number 2's right hand. Numbers 1 and 2 lift Number 3 to shoulder level. Number 3 steps on their shoulders, right foot to Number 1's shoulder and left to Number 2's shoulder.

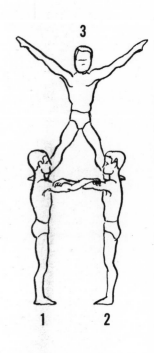

10. Numbers 1 and 2 kneel on hands and knees close to each other. Number 3 places right foot between Number 1's shoulder blades and rises to stand, placing left foot on Number 2.

11. Numbers 2 and 3 stand beside Number 1. They place their inside foot on Number 1's thighs. Number 1 grasps their upper arms. Together, they place their outside feet on Number 1's thighs. Number 1 leans back and tightens grasp on their arms. They all hold. Numbers 2 and 3 jump down.

12. Number 1 kicks up to Handstand-16 (singles). Number 3 grasps his ankle and places foot on his neck, applying pressure. Number 2, about two and one-half feet away, kicks up to Handstand and Number 3 grasps his ankle also. Number 3 places other foot on Number 2's neck. Controlling their balance, Number 3 gently rises to stand on their necks. Numbers 1 and 2 raise their heads. They hold.

Number 3 carefully steps down one foot at a time and they all return to starting position.

13. Number 1 lies on back with bent legs raised. Number 2 stands at Number 1's feet and kicks up to Shoulderstand on Feet-29 (doubles). Number 3 stands straddling Number 1. Number 1 grasps his arms. Number 3 kicks or presses to Low Arm-to-Arm Shoulderstand-28. All hold. Number 3, then Number 2 come down.

14. Numbers 1 and 2 do Stand on Shoulders (doubles)-31. Number 2 bends over and grasps hands of Number 3 who is standing in front of them. Number 1 places his hands on Number 3's waist. At a signal, Number 1 slowly lowers Number 3 as Number 2 leans forward.

15. Number 3 lies down with arms and legs raised. Number 1 grasps his hands and Number 2 his feet. At a signal from Number 1, Numbers 1 and 2 together lift Number 3 into Backbend-23 (singles). They hold. They carefully lower Number 3 to mat, reversing lift.

When lifting, bottom men must keep their arms close to their bodies. Near peak of lift, they should bend their wrists back and straighten their arms.

16. Number 1 raises Number 2 into Front Angel, Straddling Waist (doubles)-4. Number 3 places left hand on Number 2's hips and right on his shoulder blades. Number 3 kicks or presses to Handstand-16 after first applying pressure to bottom men. They hold. Number 3 returns to stand, then Number 2.

17. A—Three performers stand one behind another. Number 2 places his head between Number 3's legs and lifts him to a Seat on Shoulders (see Backward Roll to Stand on Shoulders–40, doubles). Number 1 places his head between Number 2's legs and lifts Numbers 2 and 3 to Seat on Shoulders. Number 3 hooks his feet behind Number 2 and Number 2 behind Number 1. Instead of a triple Seat on Shoulders, performers can start with a triple Thighstand (see Thighstand–16, doubles). Then proceed to triple Seat on Shoulders from there.

B—Number 2 clasps hands with Number 1 and slowly rises to a stand on Number 1's shoulders. Number 1 grasps behind Number 2's knees.

C—When steady, Number 3 clasps hands with Number 2 and he rises to a stand. Number 2 grasps him behind knees. Number 3 raises arms up. They hold.

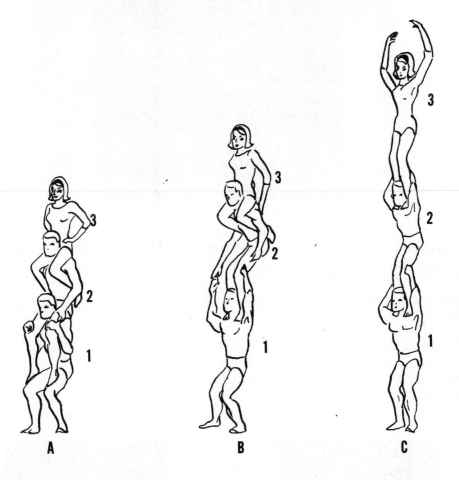

A   **B**   **C**

Recovery Methods

(1) Number 3 sits down on Number 2's shoulders and Number 2 on Number 1's shoulders. Number 3 goes to Thighstand and Number 2 a Thighstand on Number 1. Number 2 lowers Number 3 to a stand. Then Number 1 lowers Number 2.

(2) All three performers lean forward, holding behind knees. When Number 3 gets fairly close to mat, he jumps and rolls forward. Next Number 2 jumps and rolls forward. Finally, Number 1 bends forward and rolls. This should take place in a rapid, one, two, three action.

The roll recovery should be learned properly from a Two-High Stand on Shoulders. Then when Numbers 2 and 3 can fall and roll properly, they are ready for a high fall and roll recovery.

A picture of a Three-High with the spotting technique is shown on the following page.

Following are examples of four-man pyramids:

18. Numbers 3 and 4 stand facing each other. Numbers 1 and 2 stand behind and grasp them by waist and lift them to Thighstand-16 (doubles). Numbers 3 and 4 clasp each other's arms.

19. Numbers 1 and 2 do a Stand on Shoulders-31 (doubles). Numbers 3 and 4 stand beside Number 1 and raise their inside arms upward. Number 2 reaches down and clasps arms with Numbers 3 and 4. Number 1 places hands on their hips. Number 2 lifts Numbers 3 and 4 up and leans back as Number 1 lifts Numbers 3 and 4, pushing them outward.

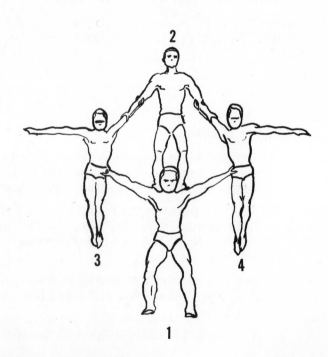

20. Number 1 lies down with legs and arms raised. Number 2 places shoulders against Number 1's feet and walks his feet forward. Number 3 kicks or presses to a Low Arm-to-Arm-28 (doubles). Number 2 lowers his arms and grasps Number 4 by arms. He raises Number 4 to his thighs; then lifts him overhead. Then Number 4 presses to a High Arm-to-Arm-58 (doubles). Number 2 lowers Number 4 to mat and Number 3 returns to a stand.

Number 4 could press to a reverse grip High Hand-to-Hand Handstand-68E (doubles) on Number 2 from a Foot-to-Hand Stand-14 (doubles) on Number 1 or be lifted by Number 2 from a stand in front of him to an L support and then to a Handstand.

Number 3 could do a reverse grip Low Hand-to-Hand Handstand-57C (doubles) on Number 1.

Practically any pyramid can be changed to make it more difficult; however, remember only do what you do well and safely.

Following are examples of five-man pyramids:

21. Numbers 1 and 2 take a push-up position. Numbers 3 and 4 kneel behind them and grasp their ankles. Numbers 3 and 4 lift their legs up and Number 5 steps up to the necks of Numbers 1 and 2.

22. Five men stand beside each other. Number 1 clasps arms with Numbers 2 and 3. They place their feet against those of Number 1 and lean sideward with straight bodies. Numbers 4 and 5 place their feet against those of Numbers 2 and 3 and clasp arms with them. They also lean sideward. This is called the Fan.

23. Numbers 1 and 2 lie with knees bent and arms raised up, elbows bent and hands cupped. Number 3 steps up on Number 1's and Number 2's hands. They straighten their arms. Number 4 places his head between Number 1's knees and grasps his lower legs. He kicks up carefully and Number 3 grasps his front ankle balancing him. Number 5 does as Number 4 and Number 3 balances him also.

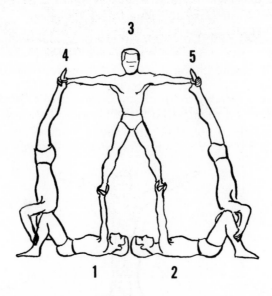

24. Numbers 1 and 2 raise Numbers 3 and 4 into Thighstand-16 (doubles). They stand close enough at first so Numbers 3 and 4 can clasp arms. Number 5 does Mount to Shoulders-31 (doubles) on another performer's shoulders. They walk toward Numbers 3 and 4. Number 5 steps off to a seat on Number 3's and Number 4's arms. Bottom man steps inconspicuously to side. He returns and Number 5 remounts his shoulders. He dismounts and Numbers 3 and 4 jump off.

Extra performer can spot Number 5 if needed.

3   1   5   4   2

Following are examples of six-man pyramids:

25. Two outside couples do Front Angels-1 (doubles). Middle couple does Back Angel-2 (doubles).

26. Middle two performers do a Mount to Stand on Shoulders-31 (doubles). Two outside performers squat down as two top men sit on their backs. Two bottom men straighten their knees. All hold.

159

Following is an example of an eight-man pyramid:

27. Numbers 1, 2 and 3 stand about two feet apart. Numbers 4 and 5 climb to a stand on their thighs. They support Numbers 4 and 5 by their waist. An outside performer walks up with Number 6 on his shoulders. Number 6 climbs off to a stand on the shoulders of Numbers 4 and 5. Numbers 7 and 8 kick to a Handstand. All hold. Outside performer returns and Number 6 steps back to his shoulders. Numbers 7 and 8 return to a stand after their ankles are released. Numbers 4 and 5 jump back. All return to a single file, facing forward.

Following is an example of a ten-man pyramid:

28. Five couples do Mount to Seat on Shoulders-40. Two sets of outside couples face each other and clasp arms. Middle couple, the tallest, remain facing forward.

Following are examples of mass pyramids:

29. a. Performers line up single file, facing onward.

b. Count One: Two from extreme left step in front of pair at their right and kneel on hands and knees. Pair at extreme right do the same. Four pull out of middle of line, and kneel down. Three others climb on their backs.

c. Count Two: At one end a performer climbs on bottom men's backs. Another stands on their hips. At other end, they do the same. From middle two men climb onto backs of three below. Last performer climbs up to stand on top two to form a middle ten-man pyramid. All hold.

Count Three: Top men jump backward. Two outside men can come down first and help top man in middle get down. Next level moves off and back. Then next level and finally, middle four promptly move back to starting position.

All pyramids should start and end this way, following count prescribed on preceding page.

Cheerleaders spend much time in tumbling and balancing and in pyramid building. Their repertoires consist of cheers, pyramid building and tumbling. Here are examples of mass pyramids employed by cheerleaders:

30. Two boys in middle back lift top girl to their right and left shoulders, respectively, and grasp behind her knees with outside hands. With their free arms they lift second girl to a stand on thighs. Both girls raise arms diagonally upward. Boys grasp free arms.

Two boys in middle front kneel down and grasp girl's legs, who is in a stride stand. They lift her to a Split-6, resting her legs on their shoulders. She raises her arms.

As they build middle section of pyramid, boys on outside lift girls to rest on their hips. Girls raise their outside arms and legs sideward. Finally, girl in front lowers into a Split.

Courtesy of MSU Sports Information Department.

162

31. Four boys stand facing forward with arms clasped. Two outside boys stand behind three girls and lift them one at a time to a seat on bottom men's shoulders.

Next they lift a girl to a stand on their shoulders. These girls step off their shoulders to a stand on girls' thighs below. Supporting girls grasp upper girls by knees.

Two boys who have done lifting now come around to side and kick to Handstand. Outside boys of middle pyramid grasp their ankles to assist them. At same time girl in front lowers to a Split.

Courtesy of MSU Sports Information Department.

Chapter 5

Advanced Individual Tumbling Routines

Now that the tumbler has learned most of the individual and doubles stunts, as well as some fundamental combinations of stunts, he is ready to begin working on advanced routines. (Routines are combinations of two or more stunts done continuously.) Practiced diligently, routines should provide the tumbler with many challenging and satisfying moments.

The routines which follow do not contain all the possible combinations of stunts; however, they do provide the tumbler with a background and knowledge for developing more of his own routines, giving him an opportunity for creativeness.

Learn the following routines in the order they are presented. However, if you have difficulty with a particular routine, after having made a reasonable attempt to learn it, pass it up for a while and move on to other routines.

1. Roundoff, Backward Handspring

A

B   **C**

A—Perform the Roundoff-19, landing on balls of feet with knees bent and arms raised forward. Throw arms upward and backward and spring off balls of feet. Thrust hips forward and throw head back to complete backward spring.

B—Snap legs down and separate them just before landing. Push off with the hands forcefully.

C—Land in an erect position with knees slightly bent and arms raised forward.

Performer must push off on Roundoff if he is to turn over forcefully. During turnover backward he should try to get his legs together for best style.

Once arms are forward after Roundoff, performer must not drop them before throwing for another backward handspring. This is different from the standing Backward Handspring.

Learning Procedure and Spotting Technique

(1) Performer completes a Snapdown-18, and lands in a preparatory sit. (See the description of the preparatory sit under Backward Handspring-40.) Spotters place their hands on his back and behind his knees as described under spotting technique-3 under the Backward Handspring. Performer does a Backward Handspring with assistance from the spotters.

(2) After learning (1) step well, performer does a Roundoff, Backward Handspring from a stand with one spotter.

(3) Lastly, he does the routine from a run as described above.

Spotters should practice placing their hands on performer's pelvis many times. Only then will they be able to shoot their hands in quickly to help performer. Spotters should get close to performer for best leverage.

If a twisting belt is used, the spotting technique is the same as for the Forward Somersault-44. If a flat belt is used, then the spotting technique is the same as for the Backward Somersault discussed on page one, fourth paragraph.

Cart Wheel-3, the Tinsica-39 or the Forward Handspring-38 with a walkout may be used to precede routine (1) above.

Keep the Backward Handspring high enough so you do not jam your wrists and low enough so you do not have to reach for the mat.

Do not lean back or dive back on the stunt; do not lean forward on take-off for this will cause you to dive forward.

a. Barani, Backward Handspring

A Barani-43 may be used in place of the Roundoff to precede the Backward Handspring; however, remember that this increases the difficulty of the combination.

Don't forget to bring the feet under the body (cut under) when landing out of the Barani.

2. Roundoff, Three Backward Handsprings (Row of Flip-Flops)

Perform the Roundoff, Backward Handspring as described under Routine 1, except this time land in a preparatory sit with arms raised forward ready to perform the second Backward Handspring. Immediately, spring over backward to perform the second handspring. Land in a preparatory sit again and perform the third handspring. This time land with knees bent slightly and arms overhead.

Use the procedure described above regardless of the number of backward handsprings you want to do after a roundoff. Keep them at the same height and speed—low and fast.

Learning Procedure and Spotting Technique

Use the same learning procedure and spotting technique described under Routine 1.

If performer overturns (overcuts) the handspring, support him on shoulder blades to keep him from diving back too far. If he underturns (undercuts), you must step in, place your hands on performer's back and leg and throw him over.

a. Barani, Three Backward Handsprings (Row of Flip-Flops)

Use a Barani instead of a roundoff to increase the difficulty of the routine.

3. Roundoff, Backward Somersault—Tucked Position (Back Sommie)

Perform Roundoff-19. Land on balls of feet with knees bent slightly and arms raised forward.

Spring upward with slight lean backward and throw arms upward and overhead, bringing knees up to hands. Throw head back and grasp legs just below knees. Pull legs over forcefully to complete Backward Somersault-45. Release grasp on legs as you see mat directly under you and land on balls of feet with knees bent and arms raised forward.

If the turn over backward stops halfway around, reach for mat and perform a handspring.

Learning Procedure and Spotting Technique

Perform Roundoff and spring for height as pictured at the left.

Spotter should stand near performer and place his hand on his shoulder blades to keep him from falling back.

Use the same spotting technique and follow the three steps of the learning procedure of the Roundoff Backward Handspring in learning this routine.

a. Barani, Backward Somersault

Use a Barani instead of a Roundoff to increase the difficulty of the routine.

4. Roundoff, Backward Handspring, Backward Somersault—Tucked Position (Flip-Flop, Back)

A   B   C

A—Do Roundoff Backward Handspring as described under Routine 1 and land on balls of feet with knees slightly bent and arms raised forward. Spring upward with a slight lean backward and forcefully throw arms overhead.

B—Lift knees upward to hands and grasp legs just below knees. Throw head back and pull legs over to complete Backward Somersault-45.

C—Release the grasp on legs and land on balls of feet with knees bent and with arms raised overhead.

Spotting Technique

Spot the somersault of this routine in the manner described under the spotting technique of the Backward Somersault-45.

The author is pictured at the right in a Backward Somersault in a Layout Position.

The spring for this somersault is the same as for the tuck somersault, but this time the knees are not brought up. Instead the hips are thrust forcefully forward as the head is snapped back. In addition, the body is held arched and the arms sideward throughout the turn over backward. Just before the landing, the performer bends his knees slightly and raises his arms overhead.

After you have learned the first eight routines rather well, work on the Layout Somersault.

The piked Backward Somersault (shown below) is also an excellent stunt. Lift the same as for a high Backward Sommie. Then forcefully pike body, bringing legs to hands. As you reach inverted position, extend body. Land with knees slightly bent.

5. Roundoff, Three Backward Handsprings, Backward Somersault (Three Flip-Flops and Back)

Do this routine in the same way as Routine 4, except this time use three Handsprings instead of one before the Somersault.

Keep the Handsprings low, fast and of the same height and drive for a high Somersault at the end of the routine.

Spot the Backward Somersault of this routine as described previously.

6. Roundoff, Backward Somersault, Backward Handspring, Backward Somersault (Back Alternates)

Perform the Roundoff, Backward Somersault—Routine 3, but this time do not spring upward for the somersault. Instead, whip it over as you would a Backward Handspring. Throw the arms directly over and under the body and arch the back. Do not place hands on mat. (The somersault is slightly higher than a handspring but just as fast; it is called a Whipback.) Also, do not grasp the legs during the Whipback; this frees your arms for a throw into the handspring which follows. Land with feet ahead of body and with arms raised forward. Immediately, throw into the Backward Handspring, Backward Somersault as if you were coming out of a Roundoff (see Routine 4). Lift the last somersault.

This routine should be performed rapidly. In fact, the routines which precede this one and those that follow should all be performed rapidly; however, control should not be sacrificed for speed.

Learning Procedure

(1) Perform the Roundoff, Three Backward Handsprings rapidly. See Routine 2.

(2) Perform the above combination, keeping hands off mat on first and third Handsprings. You are doing Whipbacks. Don't forget to whip the arms over and under the body and land with feet ahead of body and with arms raised forward.

When the performer is able to perform two Back Alternates successfully, he is ready to learn three Back Alternates. Remember the last somersault of the routine should be lifted and not whipped.

Spotting Technique

Spot the Whipback and the Handspring which follow in the same way as the Backward Somersault-45. Keep moving down mat so you are in position to spot each stunt.

7. Tinsica, Mounter

(The pictures for Routines 7 and 8 show the performer stepping on his left foot first. The author will have the performer step on his right and then his left, the opposite of what is pictured below, to remain consistent with previous descriptions.)

A

B

C

D

D

A—Perform a fast Tinsica-39, landing on balls of feet. As you step on left foot, push off with right foot and then left. Spring upward with a slight lean forward and with arms and head up.

B —Drive straight arms downward and lift hips upward, splitting straight legs and piking body.

C—Land in Handstand position with legs Split.

D—Do a Walkout, landing with legs still split. Finish with a Walkout with arms overhead and body stretched.

8. Roundoff, Backward Handspring, Backward Mounter (Arabian Walkout)

A   **B**   **C**

A—Do a Roundoff, landing with left leg behind right, knees bent and arms raised overhead.

B—Spring upward with a slight lean backward and do a half twist.

    Drive arms downward and lift hips upward with legs split. Land in a momentary Split, Handstand.

C—Complete Walkover.

Performer above is twisting to right.

<u>Spotting Technique</u> (Twisting Right)

As performer finishes Roundoff, place left arm across small of back and with thumb down, grasp performer's waist. With right hand grasp waist on his left side.

As he springs push with right hand and pull with left. As he twists, hold your left arm under his belly, and push on back to help him turn over. Support him with left arm as he lands on hands. Ease him through a Walkover.

A twisting belt can be used.

9. Roundoff, Backward Handspring with Half Twist, Piked Forward Handspring

A   B   C

C   D

A—Spring off, throwing arms overhead and pushing hips forward.

B —Land on hands and quickly push off. Twist body left.

    Land overbalanced on straight legs with body piked and arms overhead.

C—Do a Diving Piked Handspring off both feet.

D—Land with body arched and arms stretched overhead.

The backward handspring with a half twist can be done to a one-foot landing to a walkout.

10. Roundoff, Backward Handspring, Arabian Diving Roll (Backward Dive with Half Twist, Forward Roll)

A

B

B

C

A—Land with knees bent and arms raised upward.

B—Spring upward with a slight lean backward, extending body and legs, keeping straight arms overhead. Twist left a half with head, arms and a straight body.

C—Land on hands with head up and arms straight. Quickly duck head and bend arms and roll forward.

Learning Procedure and Spotting Technique

Practice this stunt on trampoline doing a standing Back Dive with Half Twist, Forward Roll. Make certain you lift your hips forward and then twist with a straight body.

Spot in a twisting belt. Ease performer into the dive roll landing.

172

Hand spot: stand on right side. As performer does dive with a half, place right arm under his belly and left hand on his back and try to ease him down through roll. This is difficult to spot.

Routines 8, 9 and 10 are directly related.

11. Roundoff, Backward Handspring, Backward Somersault, Backward Handspring, Backward Somersault (Flip, Back--Alternates)

(The first two pictures show the Backward Handspring, the next two the Backward Somersault and the last two the second Backward Handspring.)

A

B

B

C

A—Do a Roundoff, Backward Handspring as described under Routine 1. Land with the knees bent and the arms raised forward. The feet should be ahead of the body; this will keep you from leaning forward on the take-off. (Picture A shows the landing out of the first Backward Handspring.)

B—Throw a Whipback Somersault, landing again with knees bent, arms raised forward and feet ahead of body. (The three pictures lettered B show the first Backward Somersault.)

C—Whip into the Backward Handspring, Backward Somersault as described under Routine 6. Lift the somersault. (The last two pictures show the second Backward Handspring.)

The learning procedure and the spotting technique are the same as those described under Routine 6 (Back Alternates).

12. Tinsica, Forward Somersault (Tinsica, Front)

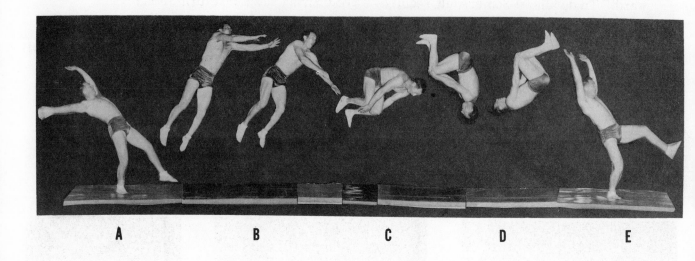

A B C D E

A—Perform a fast Tinsica-39, landing with weight on right foot.

B—Step on left foot. Push off with right and then left. Spring off with a slight lean forward and with head up and reach up with arms.

C—Bring knees up and throw head and arms down, grasping legs just below knees (tuck up).

D—Pull legs in and under body to complete somersault.

E—Release grasp on legs and land in an upright position with head and arms back and left leg raised forward ready for a Walkout. (See description of Walkout under Tinsica-39.)

Spot the somersault of this routine as described under the Forward Somersault-44.

The Forward Handspring-38, Headspring-36, Neckspring-35 or Forward Roll-1 may be used in place of the Tinsica. The Handspring may be used with a one foot or two foot take-off before the Somersault; the others are used with a two foot take-off.

The author prefers the Tinsica or Forward Handspring to the others for competitive purposes.

Pictured on the opposite page is the Roll, Forward Somersault.

The Forward Roll must be done fast and the knees must be held tight during the turn over forward. To do a good Somersault requires a good spring and a fast turn over.

a. Three Tinsicas, Forward Somersault (Three Tinsicas, Front)

Do the Tinsicas smoothly and rapidly. Use the momentum from the Tinsicas to gain added height and whip on the Somersault. The technique is the same as described for the one Tinsica, Front.

The Tinsicas can be replaced by a row of Handsprings, Headsprings, Necksprings, or Kickovers.

The Handspring Forward Somersault, Walkout, Handspring Forward Somersault can be done. In this routine the Handspring is landed on two feet. The Handsprings replace the Tinsicas in Routine 12.

A   B   C

D

E

F

G

Another variation of Routine 12 is the Forward Handspring, Forward Somersault, Piked, Diving Forward Handspring. This is pictured on the opposite page. It is an excellent Floor Exercise Event combination.

Spring off from Handspring. Lift hips into a pike and swing arms downward, bringing them toward legs. Hold piked position with hands on legs. Land overbalanced out of the piked Somersault and spring into the Forward Handspring, landing on both feet.

The legs should be together, straight with toes pointed.

This combination is the same as regular Handspring Forward Sommie except on take-off the hips are lifted forcefully.

176

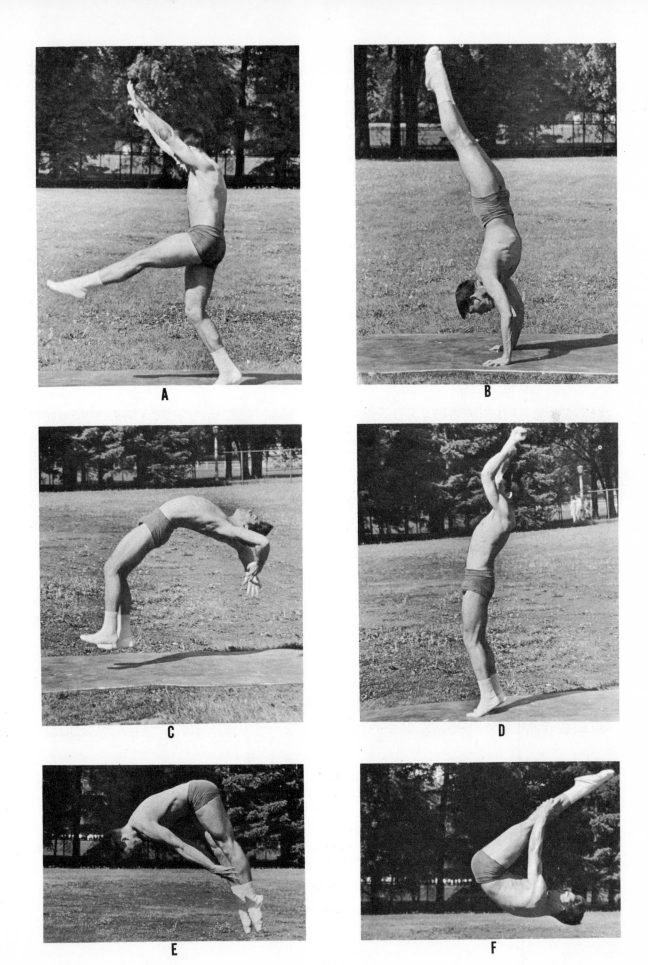

A

B

C

D

E

F

G   H

I   J

13. Roundoff, Three Backward Somersaults (Row of Backs)

Perform a Roundoff, Backward Somersault (Whipback) as described under Routine 6. Land with knees bent, with feet ahead of body and arms raised forward. Immediately spring over into another Whipback and land as described before. Then spring upward into a regular lift Backward Somersault.

Spot each somersault as described before, following the performer as he moves down mat. Watch for underturn or overturn on the somersault.

14. Roundoff, Backward Handspring, Three Backward Somersaults (Flip-Flop, Row of Backs)

A   B   C

D   E   F

Perform the Roundoff, Backward Handspring, Backward Somersault (Whipback) as described under Routine 11.

Now as pictured above, perform the other two somersaults, the one a Whipback, the last a Lift Back. (See Routine 13.) A and B show the Backward Handspring; C and D the first Backward Somersault; E and F the second Backward Somersault.

The row of somersaults may be done from a standing start.

Add a Backward Somersault with a Full Twist on the end of the row of Three Backward Somersaults and increase the difficulty of this routine.

Do not rush into the twist.

Use a twisting belt in spotting this routine.

15. Cartwheel, Sideward Somersault (Cartwheel, Side or Side Sommie)

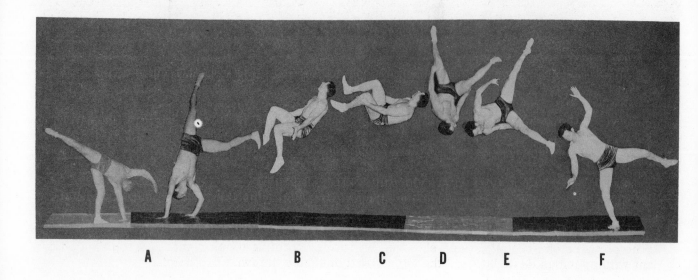

A   B   C   D   E   F

A—Perform a fast Cartwheel-3, landing on both feet. (The take-off may be made from one foot at a time or from both feet.)

B—Spring sideward off balls of feet, lifting arms diagonally upward.

C—Bring knees up toward body and grasp them.

D—Pull them over sideward and complete somersault.

E—Make certain the turn over is straight to the side. (The legs may be straightened as in picture D or they may be bent when upside down.)

F—Land on the right foot, holding the left leg sideward. This is a Walkout Sideward. See description of Forward Walkout under Tinsica-39 singles.

Do the somersault as described under Side Somersault-46 with legs straddled.

The author is pictured at the right performing a Sideward Somersault in competition.

See the Sideward Somersault-46 for the spotting technique.

a. Three Cartwheels, Sideward Somersault (Cartwheels, Side or Side Sommie)

Do the Cartwheels smoothly and rapidly. Use the momentum from the Cartwheels to gain added height and whip on the Somersault. The technique is the same as described for the one Cartwheel Side.

16. Roundoff, Backward Handspring, Backward Somersault with Half Twist (Back Sommie Half)

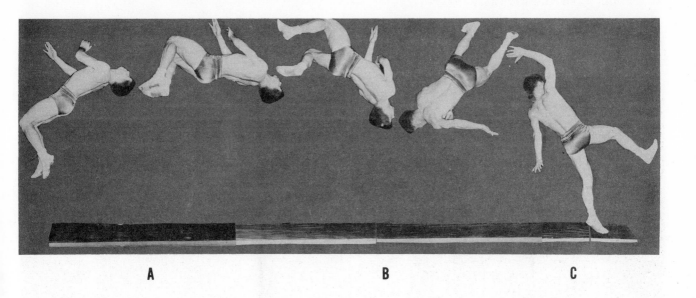

A   B   C

(The pictures on preceding page show the performer twisting to the right. To remain consistent with previous descriptions, the author will describe the twist to the left.)

Do the Roundoff, Backward Handspring, Backward Somersault as described under Routine 4; however, this time do the somersault with a straight body.

A—When you reach an inverted position, throw right arm across chest and left elbow back.

B —At the same time turn head and twist hips to left (counterclockwise) to complete half twist (180 degree turn).

C—After completing somersault, land on ball of right foot with left leg high and arms raised overhead and do a Walkout, forward.

Learning Procedure

When the performer reaches an inverted position, spotter can call the time to twist.

If performer has difficulty in twisting, spotter can call the twist as soon as the performer leaves the mat for the somersault. As his twisting technique improves, the spotter can call it later.

For a good Backward Somersault with a Half Twist, performer must wait until he almost reaches the inverted position with body straight and legs together before twisting.

Spotting Technique

Spotter stands on left side; performer twists right. As performer springs upward from roundoff, spotter reaches in and places his right arm across his back. With his left he grasps performer behind knees and throws him over. Just before performer reaches vertical position, spotter pulls in with his right hand, assisting performer with twist. Spotting technique is pictured on page 182.

17. Roundoff, Backward Handspring, Backward Somersault with Half Twist, Forward Somersault (Back Sommie Half, Front)

Do Routine 17 and land out of the half twist on balls of both feet with a slight lean forward. Immediately, spring into the Forward Somersault. This somersault is performed in the same way as the last one of a row of somersaults. See Routine 23, Tinsica, Three Forward Somersaults.

Spotting Technique

If performer overturns the half twisting somersault, reach across his body to support him. If he lands properly, spot the Forward Somersault as described before. See stunt-44, pages 79, 80 and 81.

Use the twisting belt also in learning this routine. See spotting technique under the Backward Somersault with Full Twist from a stand-45c, pages 86 and 87.

18. Roundoff, Backward Handspring, Two Backward Somersaults, Backward Handspring, Two Backward Somersaults (Alternate Backward Handspring, Two Back Sommies)

Do the Roundoff, Backward Handspring, Two Backward Somersaults as described under Routine 14. (The somersaults are Whipbacks.) Without pausing, complete the routine with another Backward Handspring and Two Somersaults.

All the stunts, with the exception of the last somersault, which is lifted, should be done low and fast.

Spotting Technique

Spot carefully all the stunts after the first handspring.

19. Roundoff, Backward Handspring, Backward Somersault, Forward Somersault (Back, Front)

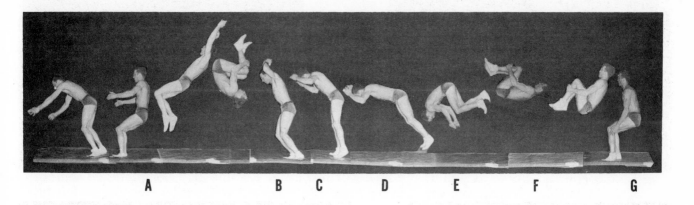

A   B C   D   E   F   G

A—Perform the Roundoff, Backward Handspring, Backward Somersault as described under Routine 4; however, this time release the grasp on the legs just before reaching the upright position. (Underturn the somersault.)

B—Shoot legs back so you land on balls of feet leaning forward with knees slightly bent and arms raised overhead.

C—Bend arms and legs.

D—Then straighten them and spring off balls of feet.

E—Throw arms down toward legs and duck head forcefully.

F—Grasp the legs, pulling them backward to perform the Forward Somersault.

G—Release the tuck when you reach the upright position and land with knees bent. Keep arms in front so you can place hands down if you overturn the somersault.

Learning Procedure

(1) Squat Jump, Dive to Handstand. Jump upward with knees bent and together with arms overhead. Land on balls of feet with slight lean forward. Spring upward again, throw straight arms downward and dive in a piked position to a Handstand. See pictures H and I on page 178.

A variation in the spring to the Handstand is in the arm throw. Throw straight arms down and back after landing out of the Squat Jump and spring upward in a piked position. Stop arms and quickly swing them under body for drop to Handstand. This is not a good preparatory stunt for the Back, Front or Handspring, Front or routines or combinations of this type, but an excellent Floor Exercise event combination.

(2) Straddle Jump, Dive to Handstand. Same as (1) above except on jump keep body fairly erect with only a slight lean forward. Raise straddled legs to a horizontal position and straight arms sideward (see picture on page 23). Land with knees and arms slightly bent and spring off the same as described above.

(3) Piked Jump, Dive to Handstand. Same as above except jump upward, bringing legs up straight and together as close to horizontal as possible with slight body lean forward. Straighten body and land with knees and arms slightly bent. Jump to Handstand.

(4) Tucked (Squat) Jump, Front Somersault. Same as (1) above except throw somersault instead of diving to a Handstand.

(5) Straddle Jump, Front Somersault. Same as (2) above except do somersault.

(6) Piked Jump, Front Somersault. Same as (3) above except do somersault.

(7) Backward Somersault, Forward Somersault from Standing start. Do a Backward Somersault landing as described above. Then jump upward and turn somersault.

Any of the steps of the learning procedure on the preceding page can be used effectively in Floor Exercise. Now you are ready to do the Back, Front at the end of the routine with spotting.

Spotting Technique

Spot the Back Somersault as described under 45 and the Front as described under 44, spotting technique 2.

Lift performer on Backward Somersault, do not try to turn him over. If you try to turn him, he may land leaning backward instead of forward.

20. Tinsica, Forward Somersault, Walkout, Tinsica, Forward Somersault (Front Alternates) (Tinsica Tigna Alternates)

Do the Tinsica, Forward Somersault as described under Routine 21. Complete the somersault by landing on right foot with left leg high. Perform the Walkout by stepping on left foot. (See description of Walkout under Forward Handspring-38.) After the Walkout complete the routine by performing the second Tinsica, Forward Somersault.

Overturn the first somersault but keep head back. This gives you momentum to carry through the second Tinsica and Somersault smoothly.

Spotting Technique

Spot the second somersault as described under 44, pages 79, 80 and 81.

21. Tinsica, Forward Somersault with Half Twist (Front Half)

Do the Tinsica-39, and without pause continue into the Forward Somersault with a Half Twist-44c.

Overturn the Tinsica to make the lift into the somersault easier. Maintain the momentum through the somersault thereby making the twist easier.

Spotting Technique

Spotter stands on left side of mat.

If performer overturns somersault, place your right hand on his back to keep him from falling back.

If performer underturns the somersault, place your left hand across his chest to keep him from falling forward.

a. Three Tinsicas, Forward Somersault with Half Twist

The technique is the same as that described for Routine 12a.

22. Cart Wheel, Sideward Somersault, Walkout, Cart Wheel Sideward Somersault (Side Alternates)

Do the Cart Wheel, Sideward Somersault as described under Routine 15. Continue into the second Cart Wheel and Somersault by doing a fast sideward Walkout.

The technique of doing this routine is the same as for the Tinsica, Front alternates Routine 20. Keep the stunts moving rapidly down mat.

Spotting Technique

Spot the second somersault as described under the Sideward Somersault-46, singles.

23. Tinsica, Three Forward Somersaults (Row of Fronts)

Do the Tinsica, Forward Somersault as described under Routine 12; however, this time do the somersault a little lower and land leaning forward and on both feet. Immediately, spring into second and then third somersault. Keep the somersaults low and fast. If possible, lift the last somersault.

Learn as many as possible of the combinations under learning procedure for Roundoff, Flip-Flop, Backward Somersault, Forward Somersault (Routine 19) before doing the Tinsica, Three Forward Somersaults.

<u>Spotting Technique</u>

Spot each somersault as described under 44a running Forward Somersault, pages 79, 80 and 81.

24. Roundoff, Backward Handspring, Backward Somersault with Full Twist (Back Full)

(The pictures show the performer twisting to the right, but to remain consistent with previous descriptions, the author describes the performer twisting to the left.) Pictures A, B, C show the Backward Handspring and pictures D, E, F, G and H, the Backward Somersault with Full Twist.

A

B

C

D

E

F

185

G   H

On take-off for somersault lift bent arms overhead. Turn head sharply left, pull bent left elbow back behind ear and drive bent right arm across chin. Turn body with legs together and
straight to left. As you pass half twist, bring arms close to body with hands in front of chest.
When you pass inverted position, complete full twist. Throw arms out to side and bend body
to stop twist and bring legs down to stand.

Do not lean back or overarch back on take-off. This action will make your somersault low
and will make twisting more difficult.

Do not do the twist in two parts. This makes for a jerky twist. Do it smoothly.

After looking to the left, do not look back to the right. This action stops the twist.

Do not lean to the right on the take-off. Make certain you push off equally with both feet.

Do not slow up the somersault to twist. Maintain the regular somersault speed; this momentum makes twisting easier.

Twisting too early will cut the height of the somersault.

Underturn the somersault slightly, this will enable you to execute the twist and to land more
easily out of the twist.

When you learn the Full well, you are ready to put a Front Sommie after it. For the method
of execution see Routine 19.

It is possible to perform two or three Backward Somersaults with Full Twists in succession.
The somersaults must be performed as Whipbacks.

Do not rush the twists; lift each somersault.

This is a very difficult routine.

Spotting Technique

Use twisting belt in manner described on pages 1 and 2.

25. Tinsica, Forward Somersault with a Half Twist, Backward Handspring, Backward Somersault

Do Tinsica, Forward Somersault with a Half Twist as described under Routine 21, keeping
somersault low and fast. Land out of Front Half with feet ahead of body, knees bent and arms
raised forward. (Do not grasp knees when doing twisting somersault.) Immediately, spring
into Backward Handspring with a forceful hip thrust. Finish routine with a fast, high somersault.

When you learn the routine well, you can add another Backward Handspring, Backward Somersault, Forward Somersault or Full Twist on last Backward Somersault.

Spotting Technique

    (1) Use the twisting belt.

    (2) Hand spot the Backward Handspring out of the Front Sommie Half.

186

26. Roundoff, Backward Handspring, Two Backward Somersaults, Backward Handspring, Backward Somersault with a Full Twist

Do the entire routine as described under Routine 18, except this time leave off the fourth somersault and lift third so you can perform Full Twist easier. The Full is thrown in the same way as the last somersault of Routine 29, alternating Backward Handsprings and Somersaults with Full Twists.

Keep the momentum going on all the stunts.

After you have learned this routine, you can do a Forward Somersault at the end of the routine or a Full and a Half Twist or a Double Twist in the somersault instead of a Full.

27. Roundoff, Backward Handspring, Backward Somersault with a Full and a Half Twist (Back Sommie with a One and a Half Twist)

Do Full and Half Twist in same way as Full Twist-Routine 24, except this time throw twist harder with head, arms and hips. Finish complete one and a half twist just beyond vertical. See fourth picture. For best form in twisting the legs should be together, knees straight and . the body extended.

Land out of twist either on both feet or on right foot with left leg high. Since landings out of Full and Double Full Twists are made on both feet by landing on one foot out of Full and Half you may avoid confusing the twists.

Don't twist any earlier and don't throw the somersault any harder than for Full Twist.

Overturn somersault slightly to make the landing out of the twist easier.

After you have perfected Full and Half Twist, instead of landing on one foot land on balls of both feet with knees bent, leaning slightly forward and arms raised upward. Without pausing spring into Forward Somersault-44b.

On this routine finish complete twist before landing and don't rush into Forward Somersault. This routine is about the same as Routine 17, Back Sommie with a Half Twist, Front Sommie.

When you land on your right foot out of Full and Half Twist and perform a Walkout, you are ready to perform without pause any of the routines described in this book out of the Full and a Half Twist.

Learning Procedure

Do Full Twist and just before landing, twist hips as far as possible to left. Each time twist earlier and earlier, throwing head, arms and upper body into it until Full and Half Twist is completed. The twist should be completed just as body has passed through inverted position.

Do not twist too early; this will cut height of somersault.

Spotting Technique

If performer should overturn the twisting somersault, spot him by placing your arm across his chest.

Use a twisting belt in the manner described on pages 1 and 2, for best results.

28. Arabian Dive with Full Twist (Forward Dive with Full Twist, Forward Roll)

A

B

C

D

E

F

Do not do this stunt until you have had trampoline, diving and extensive tumbling experience.

A—Jump upward with slight lean forward.

B—Start twist by bringing bent right arm across waist and bent left arm up behind head. Keep eyes focused momentarily on landing spot.

C—Now turn head sharply, continuing twist. At half twist your body is straight and horizontal with bent arms near chest. Legs should be straight, together and toes should be pointed.

D—Bring left arm back and right forward. Turn head so you are looking at landing spot. Complete full twist and bring arms straight overhead.

E—Land on hands with head up momentarily. Quickly duck head and bend arms in a controlled manner.

F—Do a Forward Roll to stand.

This is one of the most difficult tumbling and floor exercise stunts.

Learning Procedure

Learn it on the trampoline. First do a Jump Full Twist to Front Drop. Later do the same but duck under into a roll over forward. This can be done in the twisting belt on the trampoline. Ease performer down into roll.

Do it from a Reuther jump board, landing on a soft pile of mats. Finally, do it without the board. Be very careful.

29. Roundoff, Backward Handspring, Backward Somersault with a Full Twist, Backward Handspring, Backward Somersault with a Full Twist (Alternating Fulls)

Do a Roundoff, Backward Handspring, Backward Somersault with a Full Twist as described under Routine 24. (The Full Twist should be done as a Whipback.) Without losing speed, spring into Backward Handspring, Backward Sommie with a Full Twist. Keep the momentum going and lift the last somersault without sacrificing speed on the twist.

If you lose momentum out of Full, do two Backward Handsprings to gain speed into second Full.

Learning Procedure

(1) Do a Roundoff, Backward Handspring, Backward Somersault with a Full Twist, Backward Handspring, Backward Somersault without losing momentum on the handspring and sommie out of Full.

(2) After you have learned (1) well, do a Roundoff, Backward Handspring, Backward Somersault, Backward Handspring, Backward Somersault with a Full Twist.

(3) Finally, do Alternating Fulls.

Spotting Technique

(1) Use a twisting belt with an overhead suspension. See pages 3, 4 and 5.

(2) Hand spot the second handspring out of the Full.

a. Roundoff, Backward Handspring, Backward Somersault with Full Twist, Backward Handspring, Backward Somersault with Double Twist

Do the Full Twist as described under Routine 29 (Alternating Fulls), and the Double Twist as described under Routine 33 (Back Sommie Double Full). Learn these routines after 33, back with a double twist.

Learning Procedure and Spotting Technique

(1) Do a Roundoff, Backward Handspring, Backward Somersault, Backward Handspring, Backward Somersault with Double Twist. Use a twisting belt.

(2) Do (1) above with a Full Twist on the first somersault.

30. Tinsica, Forward Somersault with Full Twist (Front Full)

Do a fast Tinsica, Front-Routine 12. As you reach inverted position, turn head to left, throw right arm across body and left arm back and twist hips to left. Just before you reach inverted position, complete twist. Land either on right foot, ready for a Walkout or on both feet. (The landing out of the sommie will be easier if you overturn it slightly.)

Spotting Technique

Use a twisting belt. If one is unavailable, work without a belt and do a Front Sommie with a Half Twist, trying to twist other half with hips on way down. This is the technique described under the learning procedure for Back Sommie with Full and a Half Twist, Routine 27.

31. **Cart Wheel, Three Sideward Somersaults**

Do the Cart Wheel Sideward Somersault as described under Routine 15, except this time cut the height of the somersault and overturn it slightly. Spring into the second somersault, keeping the height of this one the same as the first. Overturn the second one also. Finally, do the last somersault, lifting it as high as possible. The stunts should be done rapidly and without pause.

Spotting Technique

Spot the somersaults as described under the Sideward Somersault-46.

32. **Tinsica, Two Forward Somersaults, Walkout, Tinsica, Two Forward Somersaults**

Do the Tinsica, Two Forward Somersaults as described under Routine 23. Land on the right foot with the weight slightly forward. Do a fast Walkout into the second Tinsica, Two Forward Somersaults. Keep the momentum going on this routine.

Land on both feet at the same time out of all the somersaults except the second one.

33. **Roundoff, Backward Handspring, Backward Somersault with Double Twist (Back Sommie Double Full)**

Throw the twist as described under Routine 27, Backward Somersault with a one and a half Twist except this time do an additional half twist. If you need additional time to complete the twist, bring knees up and bend at hips just before the landing. The landing is similar to that of Routine 24, Backward Somersault with a Full Twist. It must be relaxed to avoid injuring ankles.

Spotting Technique

The spotting technique is pictured above. If the performer is in trouble at the end of the stunt hold him up until he lands properly. This technique is described under 45a-Backward Somersault with a Half Twist (singles).

34. Tinsica, Forward Somersault with Full Twist, Walkout, Tinsica, Forward Somersault with Half Twist

See Routine 30 for method of performing this combination.

Do a Tinsica, Forward Somersault with Full Twist. Land out of Somersault a little over-balanced. Without losing momentum, do a Walkout into a Tinsica, Forward Somersault with a Half Twist. See Routine 21 for the technique of performing this combination.

Use a twisting belt with an overhead suspension.

35. Tinsica, Forward Somersault with a Full and a Half

Do the Full and a Half as the Full Twist, Routine 30, but throw the twist harder. Slightly underturn the somersault to insure an easier landing. The landing is the same as that of the Backward Somersault with a Double Twist-Routine 34.

Do the twist in one part.

Use a twisting belt with an overhead suspension.

36. Roundoff, Backward Handspring, Backward Somersault with Two and Half Twist (Back Two and a Half)

A   B   C   D   E

A—The performer on his spring from the handspring has already done a quarter turn.

B—He has done a three-quarter twist. Notice his legs are crossed. This happens to most when they do a great twist. Notice also his arms are close to his body, making twisting easier.

C—He has done a one and a half twist.

D—He is completing a double twist. His legs have uncrossed.

E—He is shown completing a two and a half twist on the way down. His arms are raised overhead, so he can continue forward down mat after a Walkout.

The performer is shown twisting to the right in the pictures on the opposite page. Remember the author has been describing twisting to the left.

(Photos by Jack Gould of St. Louis Post-Dispatch Pictures.)

Do the Two and a Half Twist as the Double Twist, Routine 33, but twist harder; however, do not throw the somersault any harder. Slightly overturn the somersault to make the landing easier. The landing is the same as that of the Backward Somersault with a One and a Half Twist.

Use a twisting belt with an overhead suspension.

The twisting belt, which has been recommended by the author, was invented by Charlie Pond, one of the foremost tumbling coaches in the country.

This device shortens the length of time needed to learn the twist and makes the learning of twisting easier.

37. Roundoff, Backward Handspring, Double Backward Somersault (Double Back)

(Photos by Jack Gould of St. Louis Post-Dispatch Pictures.)

Do a Roundoff, Backward Handspring low and fast. Lift arms overhead and spring upward. Bring legs up and grasp them tightly. (Notice tight tuck that performer is holding in pictures. This is extremely important.) Now drive head back and pull legs over. When you have completed two somersaults and are in an upright position, release grasp and land relaxed.

Four Points to Remember:

    (1) Lift the somersault.

    (2) Throw arms up and back hard without traveling back.

    (3) Bring knees up quickly after spring.

    (4) Maintain a tight tuck through the Double Back.

Learning Procedure

(1) Learn a Double Back Sommie on trampoline with a normal bounce. After you have learned it well, do the stunt with a fairly small bounce.

(2) Do a timer: a fast high somersault with a tight tuck. (A timer is a preparatory stunt or movement used in the learning of a more difficult stunt.) Open a little early to avoid overturning the somersault. Do not travel back on sommie.

(3) Do a Double Back Sommie in a flat belt suspended from an overhead trolley system. In addition to the belt handler, have two spotters at the place where you are going to turn the Double Sommie. They can turn you over if you need help.

If you do not have an overhead trolley rigging, use an overhead stationary rigging. Remember, do not run past the point of suspension when you turn the stunt.

(4) When you feel you are ready to do the stunt out of the belt and the coach agrees, then do it with two spotters.

(5) Finally, do it with one spotter who stands where Double Back will be done. When you reach a one and a quarter somersault, spotter should reach in and up with bent arms, placing right hand just above lower back and left behind his knees. He should support with right hand and turn you over with left.

The person who has had the most success in teaching this stunt is Charlie Pond. However, quite a few more people have had success in doing and teaching the Double Back since Pond's tumblers introduced it in competition many years ago.

Here are two important points to remember in advanced singles tumbling:

(1) From a Backward Somersault with a One and a Half Twist, the performer without stopping can tumble forward down mat. The same can be done from a Backward Somersault with a Half Twist or from a Forward Somersault with a Full Twist.

(2) From a Backward Somersault with a Full Twist, a Forward Somersault with a Half Twist and a Backward Somersault with a Double Twist, the performer without pausing can continue tumbling backward down mat.

Chapter 6

Lesson Plans

The following lesson plans are a guide. The stunts included can be taught to both boys and girls, stressing strength stunts for the former and flexibility for the latter. The same stunts can be taught to the beginner regardless of grade, varying the method of presentation and the amount of material presented. Boys may rebel against practicing flexibility stunts if they have not been exposed to them in elementary school. Their importance may be demonstrated by showing their relationship to other sports, e. g. , the split and its similarity to the position of the hurdler, the bridge as a wrestling skill, and so forth.

First Day's Plan

1. Warm-up:

Start tumbling and balancing lesson with a short warm-up, preferably running.

2. Flexibility stunts:

a. Pretzel bend

b. Bridge

c. Forward and backward leg splits

d. Sideward leg splits (straddles)

Do each one about ten times, spending less time on them as greater flexibility is developed.

3. Rolls, forward and backward:

Show their relationship to the pretzel bend used to develop back and especially neck flexibility.

4. Cartwheels:

To determine which leg a youngster wants to lead with, have them do the lame dog run. Have them bend forward, place hands down and raise straight leg backward. Then run. If they raise their right leg back, then they should do the cartwheel leading with the left leg and arm.

The above tumbling is done across mat about six at a time across a twenty-foot mat. Leave five minutes at the end for push-ups, sit-ups and squat jumps. Repeat these for as many lessons as you think are needed to develop enough strength to perform tumbling and balancing effectively.

Second Day's Plan

Review all the previous day's activities, adding a squat headstand and a squatstand if time permits. Girls may not have too much success with these at first, so move to a headstand.

Third Day

Review all again spending less time on stunts performed reasonably well. Correct faults of less capable students, using your best students as demonstrators and assistants. If time permits, let more capable students practice the more difficult which are variations of those in this lesson. Get these from the list under categories of stunts.

Fourth Day

To the previous day's lesson add the following stunts to maintain the interest of the more capable while the less capable work on older material:

1. Forward roll, come up without grasping legs to get up. Extend arms forward.

2. Forward roll, up with one leg bent and other extended forward. Shift weight to extended leg and rise to a stand, bringing arms forward and upward.

3. Forward roll, straddle legs in sitting position (if able, touch chest to floor) or place hands close to thighs and push up to a straddle stand.

4. High bridge, raise straight leg to vertical. Lower it and raise the other.

5. Cartwheel, one-handed. This is for students who have successfully performed the two-handed.

Fifth Day

Review fourth day. Capable students can do all four forward rolls in a continuous series down length of mat.

This is your start. From the categories below choose stunts to challenge the more capable. These stunts are listed in each category according to difficulty, starting with the easiest to the most difficult.

1. FORWARD ROLL CATEGORY

You have had four previously.

5. Roll, come up in piked (legs straight and together) position, placing hands beside thighs to push up.

6. Dive roll from stand. Slowly increase dive.

7. Hurdle step (step on one foot, leap and land on both). This is the preparation for a running dive or the forward somersault.

(Go on to next category before proceeding further in this category.)

8. Dive roll from run. Absorb shock on hands; slowly bend arms and duck head, rolling over neck, shoulders and back.

9. Forward somersault. Place a rolled mat across another mat. Have spotter sit on one end to keep mat from rolling. He spots by placing one hand on front of hip and other on back. He helps performer to turn over forward to a sitting position on mat.

10. Forward somersault, landing on one foot ready for a walkout into another forward direction stunt. If performer starts cart wheel with left foot, he should land on right out of the somersault.

11. Forward somersault, piked position in air.

2. BACKWARD ROLL CATEGORY

You have had one backward roll.

2. Backward roll, landing on one knee with other leg raised and back arched.

3. Back roll. Complete roll and leave hands down with one foot down, leg straight and other leg up vertically in a split (inverted split).

4. Back roll to straddled position with arms sideward.

5. Back roll to piked stand.

6. Back roll, fishflop. Grasp ankles of performer to control his roll downward.

(Go on to next category.)

7. Back roll to headstand.

8. Back roll to handstand.

9. Back handspring, standing or from snapdown or from roundoff, whichever comes easier.

10. Back somersault, same as 9.

3. CARTWHEEL CATEGORY

You have had two cartwheel stunts previously.

3. Skip step. This is needed so tumbler can start his first stunt from a fast run off one foot without losing speed. Walk forward left foot, right. Hop on right foot with left leg raised. Step down with left and do the stunt.

4. Roundoff.

5. Snapdown (mule kicks—a series of snapdowns without pause). First do it from a rolled mat to get feeling of flight. Land with hands raised forward ready for backward stunt.

6. Diving cartwheel, two-handed.

7. Diving cartwheel, one-handed. An excellent preparation for aerial cartwheel.

8. Roundoff, one-handed.

9-10. Diving roundoffs, two-handed and one-handed, similar to diving cartwheels. These are excellent preparations for barani.

Put down a rolled mat across tumbling mat. Run and dive upward, placing hands on rolled mat. Push off to complete stunt. Have someone sit on mat to keep it from rolling.

11. Butterfly.

(Go on to next category.)

12. Aerial cartwheel. Spot carefully.

13. Barani (aerial roundoff). Spot.

14. Sideward somersault. Spot.

4. BALANCE CATEGORY

You have had two balance stunts.

3. Headstand. Fall into a controlled bridge with spotting instead of rolling out for a while. This is safer.

4. Forearm headstand.

5. Forearmstand.

6. Handstand. Fall into bridge out of handstand. Don't walk when learning handstand. There are many methods of getting into a handstand.

5. FLEXIBILITY CATEGORY

You have had four flexibility stunts.

5. Backbend, placing hands on rolled mat. Push up to stand; then do it assisted without mat; then without assistance if able. Do not hurry.

6. Backbend, inside-out.

7. Backbend, crab walk.

8. Forward limberover.

9-10. Back walkover and back walkover, switch kick.

11-12. Forward walkover and forward walkover, switch kick.

13. Back limberover.

6. SPRINGS CATEGORY

1. Kip-up to bridge. Rise to stand.

2. Kip-up (snap-up) assisted. Later do without assistance after many trials.

3. Neckspring (roll, kip).

4. Headspring. Take off from both feet.

5. Forward handspring.

6. Tinsica. This is the same as a fast forward walkover with a push.

7-8. Diving tinsica, two-handed and one-handed. This is excellent preparation for the aerial walkover.

9. Aerial walkover (kickover).

10. Backward handspring. This was listed under backroll category.

11. Backward somersault. This was listed under backroll category.

Be as explicit in explaining spotting as the tumbling and balancing stunts. Teach some tumbling stunt on a trampoline. Forward and backward rolls, backward and backward extension rolls to hands and knees drop or front drop, headstand or handstand to bridgeover are all adaptable to the trampoline. Postpone teaching of the back handspring until much of the material presented before is practiced.

Another event to teach which develops naturally from tumbling and balancing is floor exercise. Floor exercise for girls consists mainly of ballet and other dance movements and tumbling and acrobatic stunts done without pause unless music lends itself to a slight pause. The music must be interpreted carefully by the performer. The tumbling and acrobatics must blend in smoothly with the dance movements. The tumbling must be executed with excellent form; the acrobatic movements must not be done with excessive flexibility. No strength stunts are permitted.

Boys' floor exercise consists of a great deal of tumbling and leaps with some movements of flexibility, balance and strength. They usually start their routine with a sequence of tumbling, concluding this way also with a different sequence. Blending with the tumbling start, are flexibility, balance and strength stunts and fundamental stunts like rolls, springs and cart wheels. Some rhythmic movements are employed to combine sequences and to help the performer change direction smoothly. This is important since the performer is required to traverse most of the required forty-by-forty foot area.

Grading and recording the student's progress is important. A good method is to use a check list for each student. The student's name and other information about him can appear at the top of the page. List the stunts as follows:

1. Forward roll   (   )
2. Backward roll   (   )
etc.

When a stunt is passed, place a check between the parentheses. If the execution of the skill is passable, but needs more work, indicate this with a question mark. When a stunt has been introduced but not tested, indicate this by placing an x before the number. For strength stunts put the number attained between the parentheses. In this way the student will know exactly where he stands. This allows him to proceed at his own level.

To help you in the development of your own combinations, the author presents examples of fundamental and advanced combinations of singles and doubles tumbling and balancing stunts:

Singles Tumbling

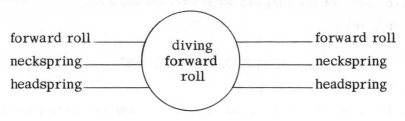

Figure 7

(The stunt in the circle is the one under consideration; the stunt on the left side is the one leading into it; while the stunt on the right is the one leading from it into other stunts. Lines leading to and from the circle show that the three stunts are connected.)

Singles Tumbling and Balancing

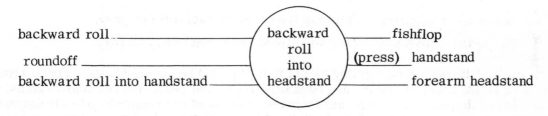

Figure 8

Singles Balancing

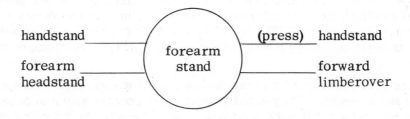

Figure 9

Doubles Balancing

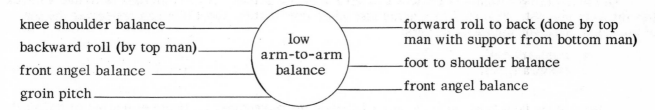

Figure 10

Doubles Balancing

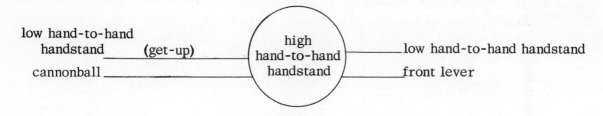

low hand-to-hand
    handstand ——— (get-up) ——— high hand-to-hand handstand ——— low hand-to-hand handstand

cannonball ——————————— ——— front lever

Figure 11

Singles Tumbling

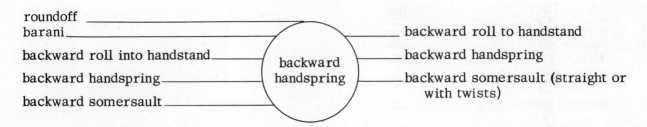

roundoff ——————————————
barani ————————————————— ——— backward roll to handstand

backward roll into handstand ———— backward handspring ——— backward handspring

backward handspring ———— ——— backward somersault (straight or with twists)

backward somersault ————

Figure 12

Singles Tumbling and Balancing

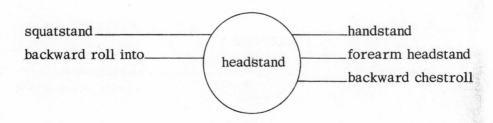

squatstand ——————— ——— handstand

backward roll into ——— headstand ——— forearm headstand

——— backward chestroll

Figure 13

Singles Tumbling and Balancing

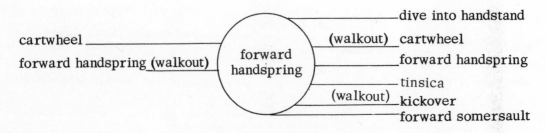

cartwheel ——————— ——— dive into handstand

forward handspring (walkout) ——— forward handspring ——— (walkout) cartwheel

——— forward handspring

——— tinsica

(walkout) kickover

forward somersault

Figure 14

200

Singles Tumbling

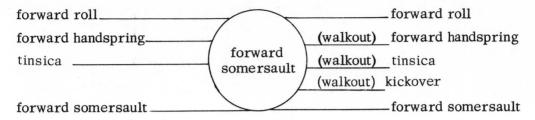

Figure 15

Singles Tumbling

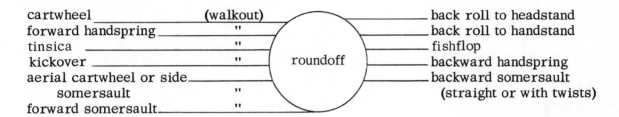

Figure 16

Singles Tumbling

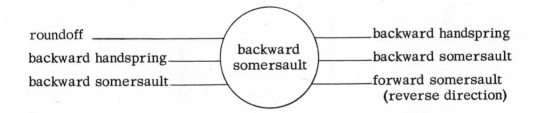

Figure 17

Singles Tumbling

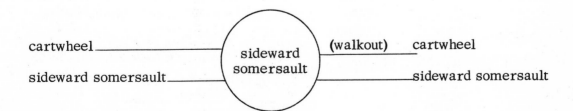

Figure 18

Singles Tumbling and Balancing

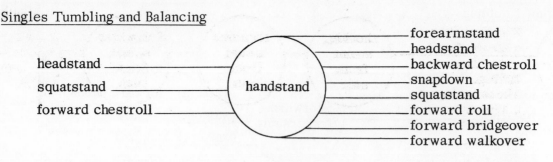

Figure 19

In order to do doubles tumbling stunts in sequence the partners have to pause between stunts, so they can change positions in preparation for the next stunt. These pauses do not detract from the combinations.

The method of combining doubles tumbling stunts is shown below:

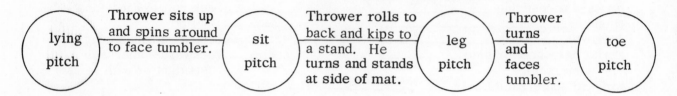

Figure 20

The above pattern is called the Pitch Series. This is a spectacular show routine if two throwers and two tumblers are used. The throwers can place themselves back to back; the tumblers can stand face to face and try to do their movements simultaneously.

In planning a doubles tumbling routine use singles tumbling stunts to change positions wherever they seem to blend into the combinations effectively. An example of this is shown above where the thrower, after having thrown the tumbler in a sit pitch, does a kip to a stand. This makes for a smooth transition into the next stunt.

Following are some more examples of doubles tumbling and balancing combinations:

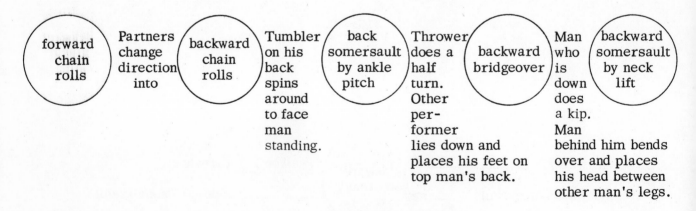

Figure 21

202

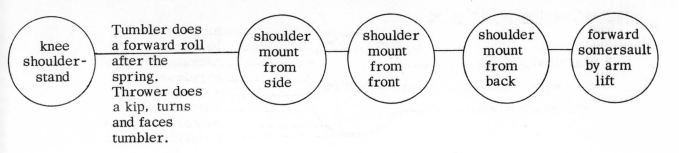

Figure 22

Chapter   7

Competitive Tumbling and Officiating

To stimulate interest in tumbling as a physical education activity or as a competitive sport, call on skilled performers in other communities to present a tumbling and gymnastics demonstration for your group. In addition, ask these people to work with and teach your outstanding youngsters.

As a follow-up take the best tumblers in your group to other communities for workout sessions with other groups.

The next step is to organize a club composed of members of all ages and both sexes. When ready, this club could take part in a physical education demonstration or circus in your school or at special functions outside school. If the opportunity presents itself, these performances could be held in other communities as well. Affairs of this type are excellent devices for displaying the physical education program to the community.

The final step is to form a tumbling team or make it a part of a gymnastics team. If skilled enough, these tumblers could compete in tournaments as a team.

The objective of competitive tumbling is for the tumbler to outperform his opponents by doing more difficult routines in a flawless manner. He is rated on a basis of 100 percent for a perfect exercise of which 50 percent is awarded for form and style of execution while 50 percent is given for the difficulty and combination of stunts. Four officials judge and award points on the calibre of performance. The high and low scores are discarded and the middle scores are totaled to determine the placings.

In championship meets, five officials are used, one is designated the superior judge while the other four perform their normal duties. The task of the superior judge is to watch for technical infraction. If this occurs, he calls a conference of the other four judges and the infraction is discussed and eliminated.

To equalize competition the following classes are established:

Novice   —11 years of age or under, or elementary school age (winner moves up to next class).

Junior   —12 years through 14, junior high school age (winner moves up).

Senior   —15 years through 17, senior high school age (winner moves up).

Championship—18 years and above, college age and above.

In national championship tournaments the tumbler is required to do four routines in a two-minute time limit.

In this competition the performer does an optional exercise of four routines. In other words, he is free to compose and perform his routines with few restrictions in any way he wishes. One of these is that he must do a predominantly forward or sideward tumbling cross down the mat as one of his routines.

In the novice and junior classes, performers should be required to do compulsory exercises. These would be graded on the manner of execution only and not on the difficulty which is already established. Some samples of required exercises are shown on the opposite page.

Novice: Routine one

    Cross one: cart wheel, roundoff, backward roll extension

    Cross two: kip, forward handspring (performed in the opposite direction)

  Routine two

    Cross one: diving forward roll, rise on one foot, roundoff, backward roll to handstand, snapdown, fishflop

    Cross two: neckspring, headspring to arched stand, lower slowly to headstand (press to) handstand (performed in the opposite direction)

Below are some suggestions for further competition:

1. Handstand walk forward for distance

2. Handstand push-ups

3. Doubles tumbling and/or balancing (consists of at least ten stunts)

Below are abbreviations which the judge can use in recording stunts and routines:

SINGLE STUNTS

FR	—Forward roll	CR	—Chestroll
BR	—Backward roll	BF	—Butterfly
C	—Cart wheel	BH	—Backward handspring
BRHD	—Backward roll to headstand	CRDL	—Cradle
BRHN	—Backward roll to handstand	FS	—Forward somersault
FF	—Fishflop	FS(1/2)	—Forward somersault with half twist
K	—Kip		
NS	—Neckspring	BS	—Backward somersault
FLO	—Forward limberover	BS(1/2)	—Backward somersault with half twist
FH	—Forward handspring		
HDS	—Headspring	BS(1)	—Backward somersault with full twist
FWO	—Forward walkover		
BWO	—Backward walkover	AC	—Aerial cart wheel
BLO	—Backward limberover	BAR	—Barani
RO	—Roundoff	KO	—Kickover
T	—Tinsica	SS	—Sideward somersault

ROUTINES

RO, BH	—Roundoff, backward handspring
RO, 3 BH	—Roundoff, three backward handsprings
RO, BS	—Roundoff, backward somersault
BOR, BS	—Barani, backward somersault
RO, BH, BS	—Roundoff, backward handspring, backward somersault
RO, 3 BH, BS	—Roundoff, three backward handsprings, backward somersault
RO, BS, BH, BS (ALT.)	—Roundoff, backward somersault, backward handspring, backward somersault
T, FS; T, TG	—Tinsica, forward somersault, tinsica tigna
3 T, FS; TG	—Three tinsicas, forward somersault, 3 tinsicas tigna
RO, 3 BS	—Roundoff, three backward somersaults
RO, BH, 3 BS	—Roundoff, backward handspring, three backward somersaults
RO, BH, 3 BS, BS(1)	—Roundoff, backward handspring, three backward somersaults, backward somersault with full twist

C, SS	—Cart wheel, sideward somersault
3 C, SS	—Three cart wheels, sideward somersault
RO, BH, BS(1/2)	—Roundoff, backward handspring, backward somersault with half twist
RO, BH, BS(1/2), FS	—Roundoff, backward handspring, backward somersault with half twist, forward somersault
RO, BH, 2 BS, BH, 2 BS (ALT.)	—Roundoff, backward handspring, two backward somersaults, backward handspring, two backward somersaults
RO, BH, BS, FS	—Roundoff, backward handspring, backward somersault, forward somersault
T, FS, T, FS, (ALT.); T, TG, T, TG	—Tinsica, forward somersault, tinsica, forward somersault: tinsica, tigna, tinsica, tigna
T, FS(1/2)	—Tinsica, forward somersault with half twist
3 T, FS(1/2)	—Three tinsicas, forward somersault with half twist
C, SS, C, SS (ALT.)	—Cart wheel, sideward somersault, cart wheel, sideward somersault
T, 3 FS	—Tinsica, three forward somersaults
RO, BH, BS(1)	—Roundoff, backward handspring, backward somersault with a full twist
T, FS(1/2), BH, BS	—Tinsica, forward somersault with a half twist, backward handspring, backward somersault
RO, BH, 2 BS, BH, BS(1)	—Roundoff, backward handspring, two backward somersaults, backward handspring, backward somersault with a full twist
RO, BH, BS(1 1/2)	—Roundoff, backward handspring, backward somersault with a full and a half twist
T, FS(1/2), BS, BS	—Tinsica, forward somersault with a half twist, backward somersault, backward somersault
RO, BH, BS(1 1/2), FS	—Roundoff, backward handspring, backward somersault with a full and a half twist, forward somersault
RO, BH, BS(1), BH, BS(1) (ALT.)	—Roundoff, backward handspring, backward somersault with a full twist, backward handspring, backward somersault with a full twist
T, FS(1)	—Tinsica, forward somersault with a full twist
C, 3 SS	—Cart wheel, three sideward somersaults
T, 2 FS, T, 2 FS	—Tinsica, two forward somersaults, tinsica, two forward somersaults
RO, BH, BS(2)	—Roundoff, backward handspring, backward somersault with a double twist
T, FS(1), T, FS(1/2)	—Tinsica, forward somersault with a full twist, tinsica, forward somersault with a half twist
RO, BH, BS(1), BH, BS(2)	—Roundoff, backward handspring, backward somersault with a full twist, backward handspring, backward somersault with a double twist
RO, BH, 3 BS(1)	—Roundoff, backward handspring, three backward somersaults with full twists
T, FS(1 1/2)	—Tinsica, forward somersault with a full and a half twist
RO, BH, BS(2 1/2)	—Roundoff, backward handspring, backward somersault with a two and a half twist
RO, BH, DBS	—Roundoff, backward handspring, double backward somersault

A GUIDE FOR JUDGING TUMBLING

(The abbreviations in this guide are explained on immediately preceding pages.)

The limits are established for a performer doing the routines properly. If he does not, he loses points from his score for form and style.

A performer must do four different routines of which at least one must be forward.

Stunts and Routines	Explanations	Evaluations
C BRHD BRHN K NS RO T	Ground tumbling (tumbling and acrobatic stunts and combinations).	40—low limit to 44—high limit (inclusive)

(To reach low limit of next bracket, do a stunt listed directly below.)

FS (running) BH (standing) BS (standing)		45—low limit to 49—high limit

(To reach low limit of next bracket, do a stunt or combination listed below.)

RO, BH FR, FS KO AC BAR BS (gainer)		50—low limit to 54—high limit

(To reach low limit of next bracket, do a routine below.)

RO, 3 BH—a row of one-handed BH adds two points to score. RO, BS T, KO C, AC BAR, BH	To reach high limit of this bracket, do four routines here.	55—low limit to 59—high limit

(To reach low limit of next bracket, do a routine below.)

RO, BH, BS H, FS FR, FS, FR, FS (alt) FS(1/2)		60—low limit to 64—high limit

(To reach low limit of next bracket, do a routine below.)

RO, 3 BH, BS RO, BH, BH(1/2), RO, BH, BS RO, BS, BH, BS (alt) T, FS—FS at end of this routine adds two points to score. C, SS—SS before this routine adds two points to score.	FS at end of any of these back routines puts performer in next bracket.	65—low limit to 69—high limit

KO or FS before all routines adds two points to score.

(To reach low limit of next bracket, do one routine on following page.)

Stunts and Routines	Explanations	Evaluations
RO, BH, BS, BH, BS (alt) RO, BH, BS(1/2) T, FS(1/2) RO, BH, BS, BH, BH(1/2), FS	KO or FS before routine adds two points. BAR instead of RO before routine adds two points.	70—low limit to 74—high limit

FS at end of routine without changing direction adds two points.
FS at end of routine when changing direction, puts performer in next bracket.

(To reach low limit of next bracket, do one routine below.)

RO, BH, BS(1) RO, BH, 2 BS, BH, 2 BS RO, BH, 3 BS RO, BH, 2 BS, BH, BS(1)—FS after BS(1) puts performer in next bracket. H, FS, H, FS T, FS, T, FS—FS at end of straight front routine adds two points to score. T, FS(1/2), BH, BS C, SS, C, SS C, SS(1)		75—low limit to 79—high limit
	SS or FS before all routines adds two points to score.	

[To reach low limit of next bracket, do RO, BH, BS(1/2), or H, FS, or T, FS before routines in this bracket, or do one routine directly below.]

RO, BH, BS(1 1/2) RO, BH, BS(1), BH, BS(1) (alt) T, FS(1/2), BH, BS(1) T, FS(1/2), BS, BS C, 3 SS T, 3 FS	SS or FS before all routines adds two points to score.	80—low limit to 84—high limit

[To reach low limit of next bracket, do FS at end of BS(1 1/2) or after BS(1) or do BS(1/2) before routines.]

[To reach middle limit of next bracket, do BS(1 1/2) before routine.]

RO, BH, BS(2) T, FS(1), T, FS(1/2)		85—low limit to 89—high limit

[To move to lower limit of next bracket, do BS(1/2) or T, FS or do a FS after a BS (1 1/2) or after a FS(1/2).]

[To move to middle limit of next bracket, do BS(1 1/2) or a T, FS(1) before any of the routines in this bracket.]

RO, BH, BS(1), BH, BS(2) RO, BH, BS(2 1/2) RO, BH, DBS T, FS(1 1/2)	The statements for the 85 to 89 limits apply to the routines in this bracket as well.	90—low limit to 94—high limit

RO, BH, BS(3)		95—low limit to 100—high limit

As a performer does a routine, check it off in the appropriate bracket in the preceding chart. At the end of his exercise by checking the chart, you will have an indication of his score.

To help clarify this guide, the following examples are presented:

If the performer does:

> Two routines in one bracket (65-69)
> Two routines in one bracket (60-64), you would probably give him a score of 65 if his form and style were ideal.

If the performer does:

> Three routines in one bracket (65-69)
> One routine in one bracket (60-64), you would probably give him a score of 67.

If the performer does:

> Three routines in one bracket (65-69)
> One routine in one bracket (55-59), you would probably give him a score of 65.
> (The only forward routine this tumbler could do was a T, KO.)

If the performer does:

> One routine in one bracket (65-69)
> Three routines in one bracket (60-64), you would probably give him a score of 65.
> He has done one routine in (65-69) bracket which moves him to lower limit of this bracket.

If the performer does:

> Four routines in one bracket (75-79), you would give him 79.

If performer touches mat with hands or sits down after completing a stunt, he should receive credit for the stunt and a deduction of two points made from his score.

If performer lands controlled out of a twisting somersault but has not completed the twist, he should receive credit for the amount of twist and a deduction of two points from his score.

If performer uses additional tinsicas or handsprings in forward alternates or an extra backward handspring in back alternates to regain his speed out of a somersault, two points should be deducted from his score.

For a bad miss, deduct five points from the final score; for a slight miss deduct two points. Use an x to show a missed stunt.

If performer completes a routine but lands with one foot off side of mat, just one point should be deducted for this minor infraction.

If performer completes a routine but lands off side of mat with both feet, three points should be deducted from his final score.

No deduction should be made if performer tumbles off either end of the mat.

If two performers do about the same routines, then you decide which one is better by carefully comparing their style, speed and height of somersaults and by deducting for breaks in form, improper landings, low somersaults where height is desired, uneven speed, slow speed, uncontrollability, and so forth.

A spotter is permitted to stand by the mat during a tumbler's performance; however, if he assists the performer, no credit should be given for his attempt. This regulation discourages foolhardy attempts.

*** GOOD LUCK TO ALL ——— HAVE FUN ***

NOTES

NOTES